DODGE WC54 AMBULANCE

CASEMATE | ILLUSTRATED | SPECIAL

UNITED STAT
ARMY

CASEMATE | ILLUSTRATED | SPECIAL

DODGE WC54 AMBULANCE

FABIEN RAUD

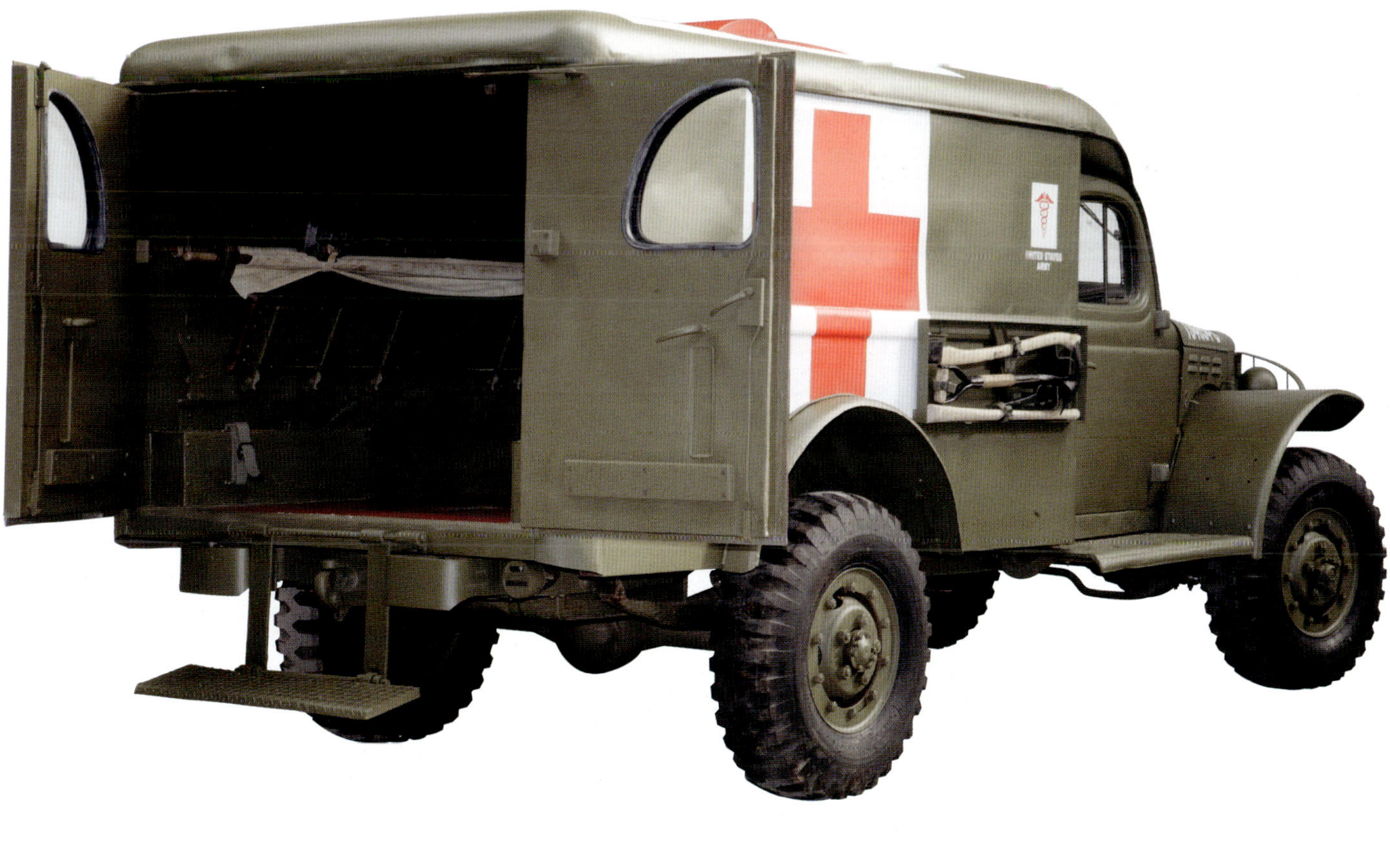

I would like to dedicate this book to my mother who always backed me in my projects and who, unfortunately, wasn't able to see this one finished.

CISS0014

Published in the United States of America and Great Britain in 2022 by
CASEMATE PUBLISHERS
1950 Lawrence Road, Havertown, PA 19083, USA
and
The Old Music Hall, 106–108 Cowley Road, Oxford OX4 1JE, UK

This book is published in cooperation with, and under license from Forties Factory. Originally published in French as *Dodge WC54: Connaissance et Restauration* by Fabien Raud, Forties Factory, 2021

Hardback Edition: ISBN 978-1-63624-213-2
Digital Edition: ISBN 978-1-63624-214-9

A CIP record for this book is available from the British Library

Design by Myriam Bell
Translated by Alan McKay

Printed and bound in the Czech Republic by FINIDR s.r.o.

For a complete list of Casemate titles, please contact:

CASEMATE PUBLISHERS (US)
Telephone (610) 853-9131
Fax (610) 853-9146
Email: casemate@casematepublishers.com
www.casematepublishers.com

CASEMATE PUBLISHERS (UK)
Telephone (01865) 241249
Email: casemate-uk@casematepublishers.co.uk
www.casematepublishers.co.uk

Images are from author's collection unless otherwise credited.

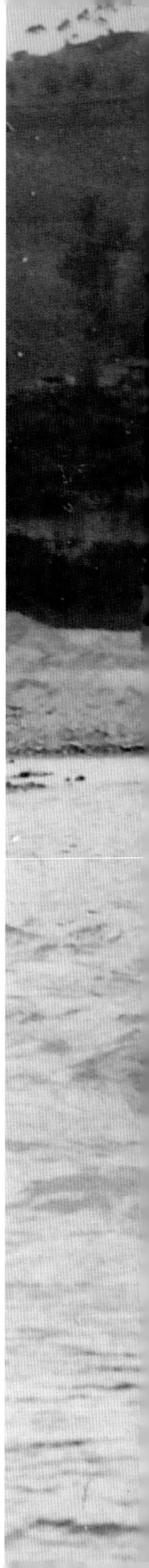

Contents

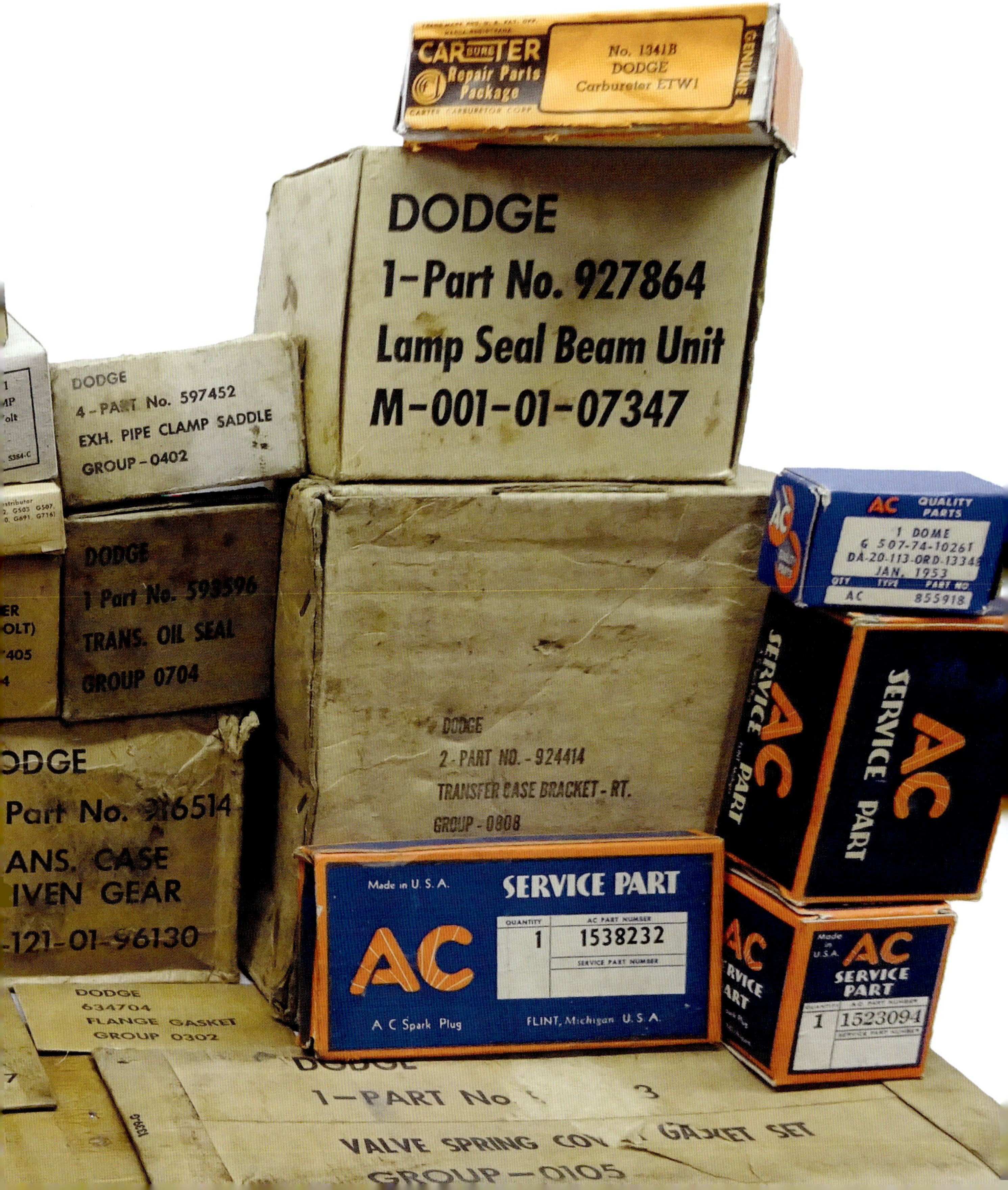
CARTER
Repair Parts Package
No. 1341B
DODGE
Carbureter ETW1
GENUINE
DODGE
1-Part No. 927864
Lamp Seal Beam Unit
M-001-01-07347
DODGE
4-PART No. 597452
EXH. PIPE CLAMP SADDLE
GROUP-0402
DODGE
1 Part No. 593596
TRANS. OIL SEAL
GROUP 0704
DODGE
2-PART NO.-924414
TRANSFER CASE BRACKET-RT.
GROUP-0808
AC QUALITY PARTS
1 DOME
JAN. 1953
AC 855918
AC SERVICE PART
Made in U.S.A.
SERVICE PART
AC
1 1538232
A C Spark Plug
FLINT, Michigan U.S.A.
AC SERVICE PART
1 1523094
ODGE
Part No.
ANS. CASE
IVEN GEAR
DODGE
634704
FLANGE GASKET
GROUP 0302
1-PART No.
VALVE SPRING COV GASKET SET
GROUP-0105

Foreword

I decided to write this book to share my love of Dodge WC54 ambulances with collectors and owners. As they are keen to carry out good restorations, the aim of this book is to help them to know their Dodge ambulance better by showing them the range of specific parts that make up this vehicle.

Restoring my WC54 ambulance was spread out over a period of some 15 years. As I didn't have any detailed documentation, I did a lot of research in the technical journals (TM—Technical Manuals, SNL—Standard Nomenclature Lists) and books dealing with the Dodge. I used period photos and a lot of documents that now contribute to the book.

This documentary research was necessary, but it wasn't enough because of the vehicle's particularities. Certain parts are specific to the ambulance. These rare parts are often missing or have been seriously damaged and are, therefore, hard to replace. Original NOS (New Old Stock) parts were sought all over the world so the vehicle could be completed. Some of them just couldn't be found as NOS and the original manufacturers no longer produce them. Using original examples and/or dimensions found in the technical journals, I was able to reproduce the missing parts or those too damaged to be used. Restoring the ambulance was therefore completed as close as possible to what came out of the factory.

As the project progressed, I decided to share my experience with other buffs who, like me, were constantly looking for *the* part that would give back the vehicle's original soul. I therefore created my own company—USMTWT (US Military Trucks, Wheels and Tracks)—specializing in selling spare parts for American military vehicles from the last world war. The aim was to find spare parts for these vehicles so they'd be available for buffs through our website or various exchanges.

This book deals with all the known particulars of the Dodge WC54. We have concentrated on the specific elements and details that make up the vehicle's complexity. We have not gone into the general mechanics common to all Dodge WCs, since these are covered very well in the technical manuals.

Introduction

History

In 1939, the Quartermaster Corps, in charge of dealing with the specifications and the production of American military equipment, started studying the development of an ambulance-type vehicle capable of going out into the field (Field Ambulance). A 4 x 4 motorized chassis in the 1.5-ton class was chosen, the one put forward by Dodge. In 1941, answering the requirement for a special emergency vehicle to equip the U.S. Army, the Chrysler Company started producing its Model WC9, which greatly resembled the WC18 and WC27. All three were classified in the ½-ton category, each having a different engine and other particularities. They were part of the WC G-505 series of vehicles built by Dodge up to 1942. The firm produced 2,288 WC9s, 1,944 WC18s, and 2,579 WC27s.

The Dodge WC54 ¾-ton ambulance followed the WC27 in 1942. It was a four-wheel-drive vehicle from the light WC range, developed by Chrysler. Its chassis was from the same family as that of the Dodge WC series. The vehicle was powered by a six-cylinder gasoline engine. The body, specific to the ambulance model, was made by the Wayne Company in Richmond, Indiana, USA. The WC54 became the standard ambulance for the U.S. Army during World War II.

Ambulance deliveries started in 1942. Fewer than 10% of the Dodge WC chassis production (255,173 built from 1942 to 1945) were intended to be ambulances. Production ceased with the last delivery of 436 units in April 1944. A total of 26,002 ambulances were built after May 1942.

The majority of the vehicles were supplied to the U.S. Army. They also equipped the British Royal Army Medical Corps, the American Field Service (AFS) and the Free French Forces.

General Leclerc's 2e Division Blindé (2nd Armored Division or 2e DB) and General de Lattre de Tassigny's First French Army used the WC54. The French Army ambulance teams were mainly staffed by women. In the 2e DB, these women were known as "Rochambelles" in the 13e Bataillon Médical and "Marinettes" in the Régiment blindé de fusiliers-marins (armored naval infantry regiment).

The vehicle's crew consisted of two people: a driver and a team commander. The driver was responsible for the vehicle, performing basic maintenance to keep it operational. The commander was responsible for the missions assigned to the vehicle as well as its logistics.

Above: U.S. Medical Field Service School, Carlisle Barracks, Pennsylvania: the new 64KD ambulance, replacement for the WC54. (*National Library of Medicine*)

Right: Manila, 1945. A new Dodge 64KD unloads a C-46 Commando while a WC54 waits its turn. (*National Library of Medicine*)

Opposite, left: Front left view without blackout lamps.

Opposite, right: Front left view with blackout lamps.

Below: A Dodge WC27, one of the WC 54's precursors.

Bottom: Great Dunmow, Essex, England, 5 October 1943. Ambulances from the 70th Service Group waiting for B-26 Marauder medium bombers of the 386th Bomb Group to return. (*RAF*)

The Dodge ambulance could carry four stretcher cases or seven walking wounded, sitting on fold-down benches.

The ambulance's task was transport, not first aid. It carried no particular medical equipment. It was fitted with four stretchers, blankets, and arm and leg splints. It moved the wounded to first aid posts or other methods of medical evacuation (such as aircraft). It was mainly used in its ambulance configuration. As the vehicle was relatively rare in service, very few were diverted to other uses. Troop transport vehicles like GMCs, Dodge 51s, and a number of others were converted into ambulances to make up for the lack of WC54s.

The Dodge was assigned to many U.S. Army Corps units, like the Mobile American Red Cross Club, the Mobile Library, and the Mobile Radio. To date, however, it is not known if any WC54s were assigned to the Signal Corps. Indeed, this unit was equipped with a variety of vehicles, like GMCs or the Chevrolet K51 Panel Truck, for its different needs.

Some Dodge WC54s equipped with loudspeakers were assigned to the Psychological Warfare Service. The Military Police also used a few in the 1950s during the occupation of Germany.

Before the end of the war, the WC54 ambulance was replaced by the WC64KD; 3,500 examples were built with better technical characteristics overall. Indeed, the body volume was greater and made of wood, which was more readily available at the end of the conflict. The suspension was improved by fitting Monroe telescopic shock absorbers. WC64KD production started in January 1945 and the vehicle was deployed just before the end of the war. The U.S. Army used the new design intensively during the Korean War.

After the war ended in 1945, the United States handed over thousands of WC54 ambulances to its European allies as part of Lend-Lease agreements, enabling them to re-equip with military material. These tough vehicles remained in service into the 1960s in Austria, Belgium, France, Greece, Holland and Norway.

Build Card

The Build Card (or Building Card) was the identity document for each vehicle. It accompanied the vehicle along the assembly line until the final check. The main information, like the serial number, and the engine and body numbers, was listed so the vehicle could be easily identified.

The date produced mentioned on the card corresponded to the date at which the last check was made at the end of the production process, whereas the date inscribed on the vehicle's identification plate corresponded to the date it was delivered to the Army.

Given a vehicle might be stored for a short while, or not pass its final check, the time gap between the two dates might run from a few days to several weeks, between the date when it was certified at the end of the assembly line and the date it was actually delivered to the Army.

The number 39 indicated the type of bodywork. On the bottom line were the date, chassis number, engine block number and the bodywork number.

Left: These "Doughnut Dollies" were assigned to the 45th Infantry Division, the WC54 being diverted from its original function as an ambulance.

Above: Stuttgart, Germany, 1955. A WC54 used as a Military Police vehicle.

Above right: Italy, late 1944. This ambulance was assigned to an American Red Cross Club mobile jazz band. (*NARA*)

Right: WC54s waiting to be delivered. (*Signal Corps*)

Right, inset: A Chevrolet K51 assigned to the Signal Corps.

Below: Saint-Malo, France, 9 August 1944. This vehicle has been diverted from its original use by installing loudspeakers and radio-communication aerials, enabling messages to be broadcast to German forces. This vehicle was assigned to the Headquarters of the 3rd Mobile Radio Communications Company. Note the 25-inch star. (*NARA*)

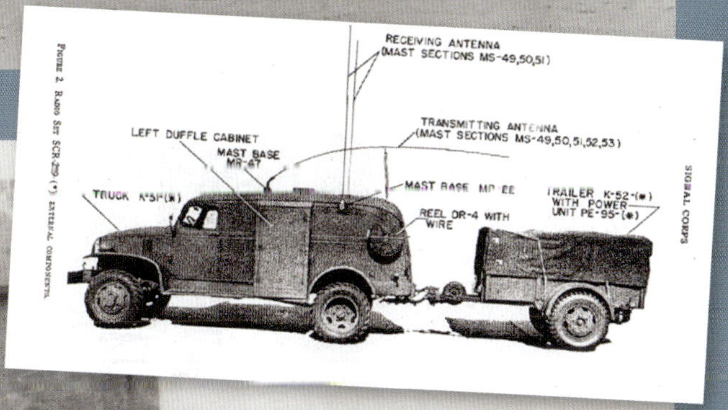

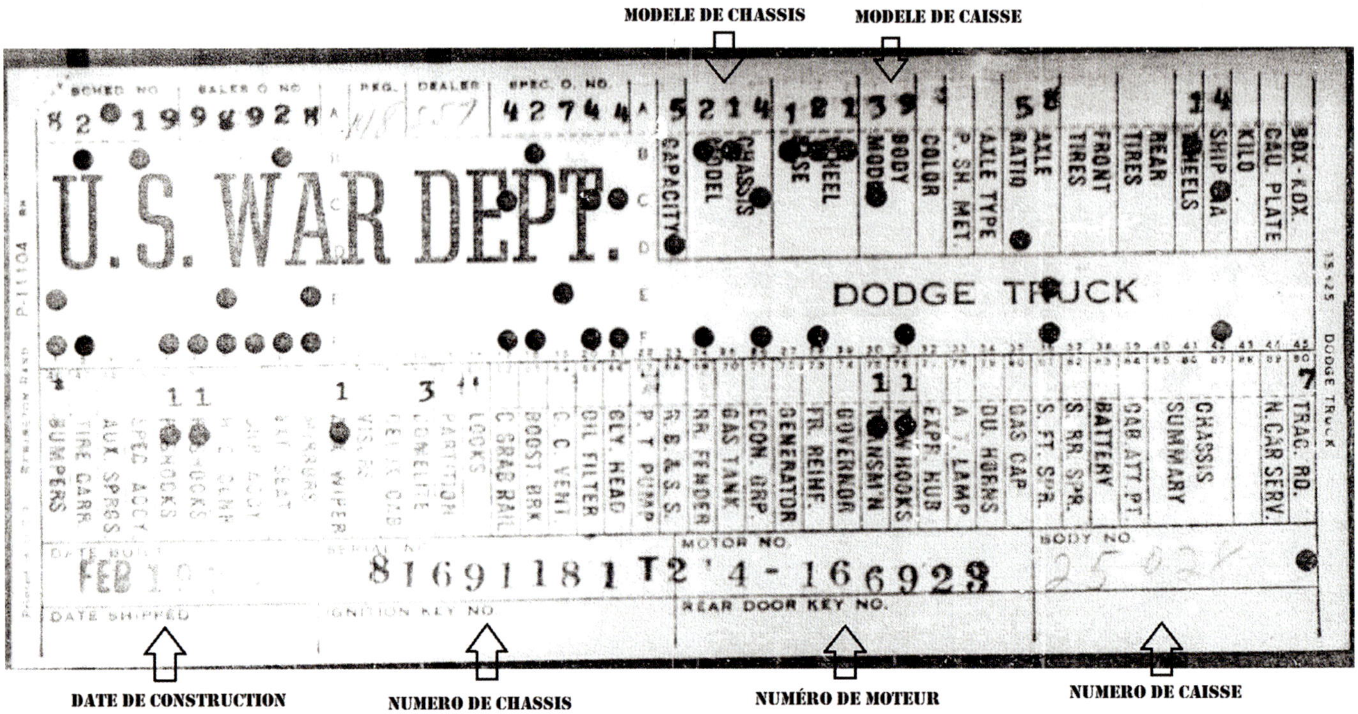

An example of a WC54 Build Card for a late production vehicle.

This document was available from Chrysler's historical service. It is obviously only delivered to owners of these vehicles.

General features

The Dodge WC54 was one of the series of so-called ¾-ton vehicles. It weighed 2.6 tons empty for a payload of 1,500 lb. It was powered by a T214 3,800-c.c., six-cylinder inline engine, rated at 92 bhp at 3,200 rpm, enabling it to reach a top speed of 55 mph. Its fuel tank held some 30 gallons, giving it a range in normal traffic conditions of 248 miles, or a consumption rate of some 8.26 mpg.

The WC54 was fitted with a gearbox made by New Process Gear, with four forward and one reverse gears. It had four-wheel drive. The ¾-ton range did not have a low-ratio transfer box unlike the 6 x 6 1½-ton models.

WC54 Ambulance details

All the items that make up the Dodge WC range are referenced in Standard Nomenclature List G657. The parts references for Dodge start with the prefix "CC" (Chrysler Corporation).

You will see later that the same part can have two references. Indeed, the classification used by the SNL differs sometimes from the one used in the catalogue from Wayne, the builder of the bodywork.

The WC54 ambulance went through several modifications and developments during its career, particularly in February 1943. The chassis numbers, and certain series of chassis numbers, indicate these modifications.

Some parts were stamped with the monogram "DPCD" which corresponds with the builder's four makes: Dodge Plymouth Chrysler Desoto.

Below and right: Examples of Chrysler's typical markings.

TM 9-2800

SECTION XI—AMBULANCES

AMBULANCE, ¾-TON, 4 x 4

GENERAL DATA

Crew			2
Weight	Net	(lb)	5,920
	Payload	(lb)	1,800
	Gross	(lb)	7,720
Shipping dimensions	(cu ft) 790	(sq ft) 105	
Tires	Ply . . . 8	Size . . . 9.00 x 16	
Tread, center to center		(in.)	64¾
Ground clearance		(in.)	10⅝
Electrical system		(volts)	6
Capacities	Fuel, 72 octane gasoline	(gal)	30
	Cooling system	(qt)	8
	Crankcase (refill)	(qt)	5
Brakes		Hydraulic	

PERFORMANCE

Maximum gradability		(percent)	54
Turning radius (ft)	Right 24	Left 26	
Fording depth		(in.)	34
Angle of approach		(deg)	53
Angle of departure		(deg)	24
Fuel consumption, average conditions		(miles per gal)	8
Cruising range, average conditions		(miles)	240
Maximum allowable speed		(mph)	54
Number of speeds forward			4

ENGINE

Manufacturer	Dodge	Model T214	
Type	In-line, 4 cycle	Number of cylinders	6
Displacement		(cu in.)	230.2
Governed speed		(rpm)	3,200
Brake horsepower			76
Ignition type		Battery	

ADDITIONAL DATA

357

Above and right: Technical specifications of the Dodge WC54.

TM 9-2800

STANDARD MILITARY MOTOR VEHICLES

AMBULANCE, ¾-TON, 4 x 4

Technical Manuals: TM 10-1531. Parts List: SNL G-502

Manufacturer: Dodge Brothers Corp. (Div. of Chrysler Corp.)

RA PD 66315

Classification: Standard

Purpose: To transport sick and wounded personnel.

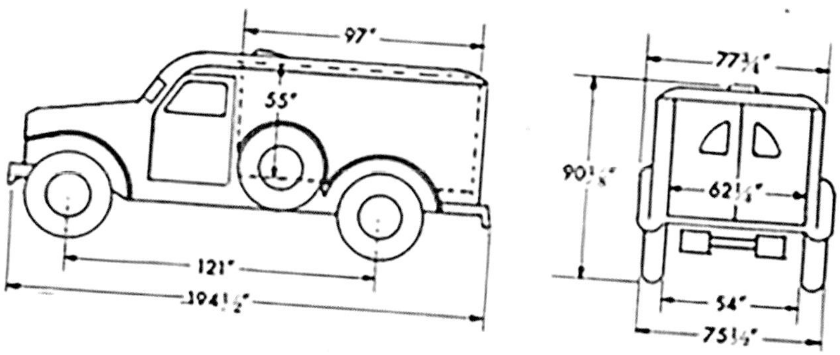

356

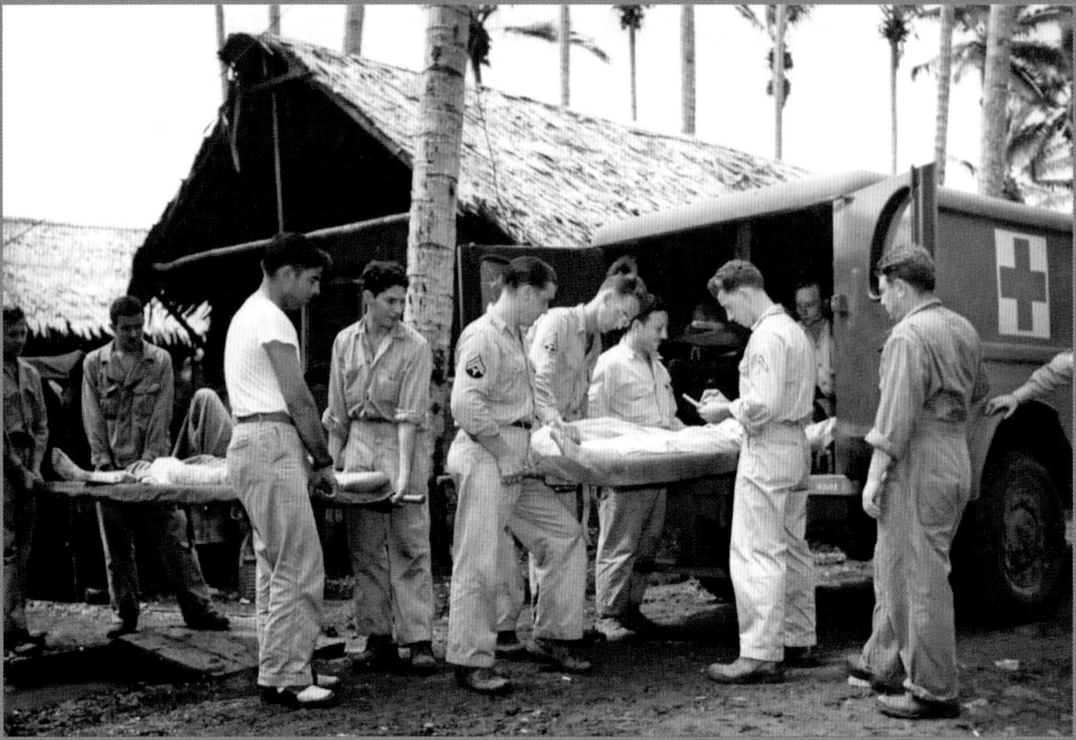

Right and below: Medical personnel load wounded into ambulance on Guadalcanal, 1944. (*USAF*)

Left: Wounded personnel being transported between aircraft and ambulances in Hawaii, 1944. (*US Army*)

Below: Wounded personnel being transported to aircraft from ambulances for medical evacuation from Guadalcanal. (*USAF*)

1 Chassis and Running Gear

Serial number

The serial number of the vehicle was stamped on the front left-hand side of the chassis. There is often a double stamp. The chassis numbers follow each other in the production of the ¾-ton chassis and are not specific to the WC54 model.

Chassis characteristics

The chassis was 194½ inches (4.94 meters) long. It was longer than that of the WC51 (166 inches—4.24 meters).

The chassis was referenced by the part number CC922021. The reference was stamped on the rear step bracket, on the driver's side.

Engine number

Every engine had a serial number. It was always preceded by the prefix "T214," for the ¾-ton series, followed by its individual serial number. It was found on the front left-hand side of the engine.

This shot, dated January 1944, shows mechanics servicing an engine, confirming the application of cream-white paint to the block. (*NARA*)

Engine block color

The color of the engine block was cream-white. This color was the same for the whole series of Dodge WC ¾-ton vehicles.

Air filter

The CC924230 air filter was the standard model, made by AC Delco, a General Motors Company. This was replaced from chassis 81705481 onwards in mid-April 1944. The new air filter model had a mesh surround, the filtering element bearing the part number CC927611. It seems, however, that at the time of this chassis number, the WC54 was no longer being produced and, as a result, this modification was not carried out.

Front and rear differentials

There were two types of differentials on the WC ¾-ton range of vehicles. The bodies and the differentials were the main differences.

- The first, so-called "simple," type is recognizable by its bolted flange.
- The second, so-called "reinforced," type has a welded flange. It was used from chassis 81657582 (beginning of March 1943) onwards except for the series 81674101–81674747.

Transfer box

The Dodge WC54 ambulance, like the other 4 x 4s in the range, was only fitted with a transfer box that had no low-ratio gears.

It had a specific propeller shaft (the part reference being CC924656).

Leaf springs

The ambulance's leaf springs were specific to the model. So as to improve the vehicle's ride, grease

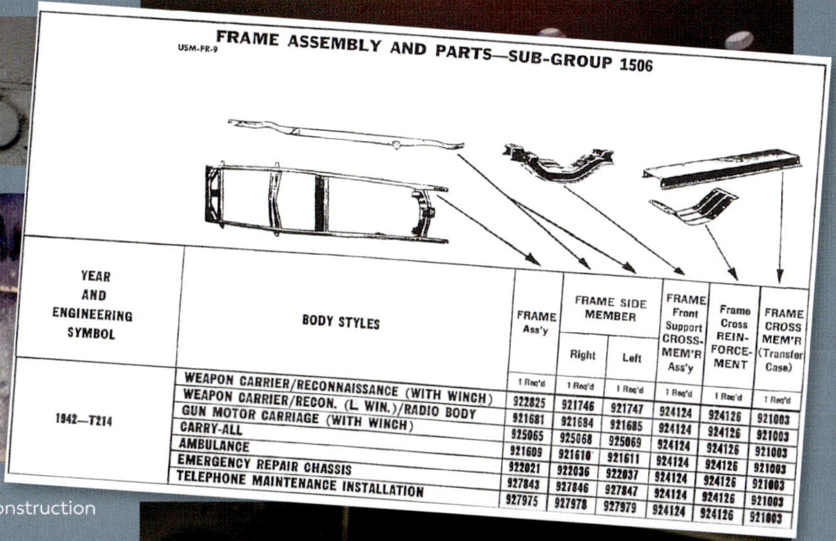

USM-FR-9

FRAME ASSEMBLY AND PARTS—SUB-GROUP 1506

YEAR AND ENGINEERING SYMBOL	BODY STYLES	FRAME Ass'y	FRAME SIDE MEMBER		FRAME Front Support CROSS-MEM'R Ass'y	Frame Cross REIN-FORCE-MENT	FRAME CROSS MEM'R (Transfer Case)
			Right	Left			
		1 Req'd	1 Req'd	1 Req'd	1 Req'd	1 Req'd	1 Req'd
1942—T214	WEAPON CARRIER/RECONNAISSANCE (WITH WINCH)	922825	921746	921747	924124	924126	921003
	WEAPON CARRIER/RECON. (L. WIN.)/RADIO BODY	921681	921684	921685	924124	924126	921003
	GUN MOTOR CARRIAGE (WITH WINCH)	925065	925068	925069	924124	924126	921003
	CARRY-ALL	921609	921610	921611	924124	924126	921003
	AMBULANCE	922021	922036	922037	924124	924126	921003
	EMERGENCY REPAIR CHASSIS	927843	927846	927847	924124	924126	921003
	TELEPHONE MAINTENANCE INSTALLATION	927975	927978	927979	924124	924126	921003

Top: A chassis with a double stamp, probably done during reconstruction by ERGM (Etablissement de Réserve Générale du Matériel, an organization that rebuilt surplus military vehicles for further use).

Above center: Engine block number: "T214" followed the engine's individual number.

Above: Note the original color of the engine block preserved under a small reconstruction plate. No other coat of paint is visible underneath.

Top right: Chassis part number.

Above right: Extract from SNL G657 presenting the chassis reference number.

Right: AC model air filter.

Below: "Simple" differential.

Bottom right: "Reinforced" front differential.

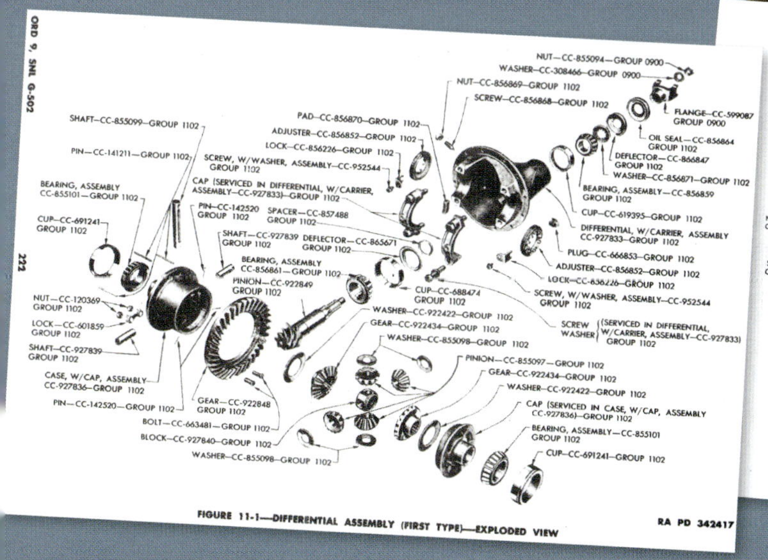

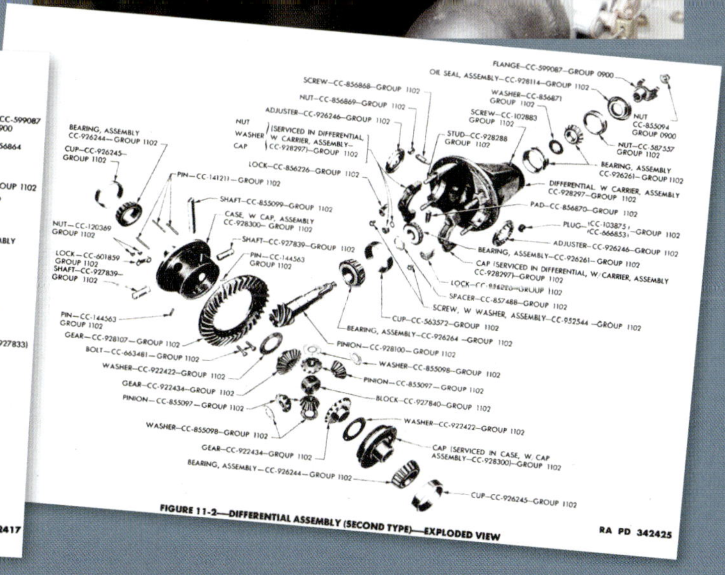

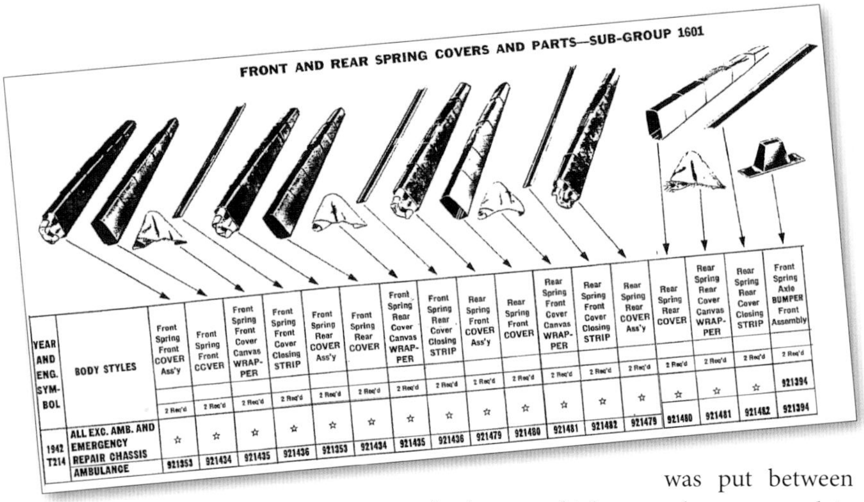

FRONT AND REAR SPRING COVERS AND PARTS—SUB-GROUP 1601

YEAR AND ENG. SYM-BOL	BODY STYLES	Front Spring Front COVER Ass'y	Front Spring Front COVER	Front Spring Front Cover Canvas WRAP-PER	Front Spring Front Cover Closing STRIP	Front Spring Rear COVER Ass'y	Front Spring Rear COVER	Front Spring Rear Cover Canvas WRAP-PER	Front Spring Rear Cover Closing STRIP	Rear Spring Front COVER Ass'y	Rear Spring Front COVER	Rear Spring Front Cover Canvas WRAP-PER	Rear Spring Front Cover Closing STRIP	Rear Spring Rear COVER Ass'y	Rear Spring Rear COVER	Rear Spring Rear Cover Canvas WRAP-PER	Rear Spring Rear Cover Closing STRIP	Front Spring Axle BUMPER Front Assembly
		2 Req'd	2 Req'd	2 Req'd	2 Req'd	2 Req'd	2 Req'd	2 Req'd	2 Req'd	2 Req'd	2 Req'd	2 Req'd	2 Req'd	2 Req'd	2 Req'd	2 Req'd	2 Req'd	2 Req'd
1942 T214	ALL EXC. AMB. AND EMERGENCY REPAIR CHASSIS	☆	☆	☆	☆	☆	☆	☆	☆	☆	☆	☆	☆	☆	☆	☆	☆	921394
	AMBULANCE	921353	921434	921435	921436	921353	921434	921435	921436	921479	921480	921481	921482	921479	921480	921481	921482	921394

Above: Elements making up the leaf springs' "envelope." "Ass'y" means "assembly," i.e., a complete component.

was put between the leaves, which were then wrapped in leather. The whole unit was then covered with sheets of folded metal; these held the leather in place and isolated it, preventing particles from outside (sand, gravel, etc.), which, if mixed with the grease, would create an abrasive paste causing the leaves to wear before their time.

The front leaves bore the part number CC921355, the rear ones CC921477.

The rear leaf springs had a rubber stop (CC916822) held in place by the assembly flanges for the differential and the leaves.

The front leaves were also dampened by a rubber stop—CC921192. There was also a stop fixed onto the chassis at the rear of the leaf, up to chassis 81656400, and also for the series 81674101–81674682. The stops were rubber but later made of steel and were omega shaped.

Shock absorbers

As well as leaf springs, the vehicle was fitted with hydraulic suspension. The small, forked connecting rods were fitted at the beginning of production. They were replaced by cone-shaped connecting rods, mounted on vehicles from 81632103 (mid-March 1943).

Exhaust pipe

The exhaust pipe, positioned after the muffler, was longer than the current models of the WC series. Its part number was CC923483.

Braking system

The braking system was the same as all the other models in the WC series. The only specifics were:

- The pipe going from the three forward connecting lines towards the rear flexible hose (CC925584).
- The longer rear flexible hose (CC922420) allowed for greater suspension clearance.

Below: Details of the elements making up the hydraulic arm suspension.

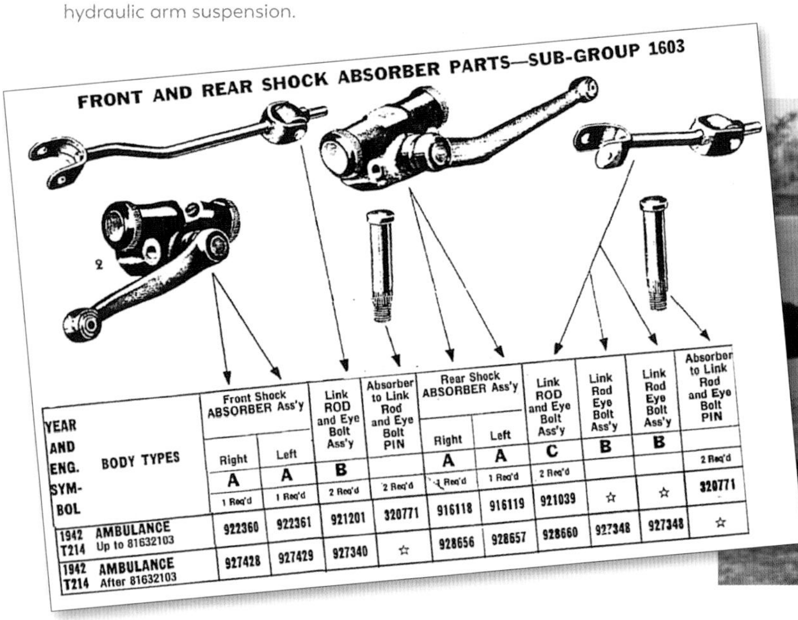

FRONT AND REAR SHOCK ABSORBER PARTS—SUB-GROUP 1603

YEAR AND ENG. SYM-BOL	BODY TYPES	Front Shock ABSORBER Ass'y Right	Front Shock ABSORBER Ass'y Left	Link ROD and Eye Bolt Ass'y	Absorber to Link Rod and Eye Bolt PIN	Rear Shock ABSORBER Ass'y Right	Rear Shock ABSORBER Ass'y Left	Link ROD and Eye Bolt Ass'y	Link Rod Eye Bolt Ass'y	Link Rod Eye Bolt Ass'y	Absorber to Link Rod and Eye Bolt PIN
		A	A	B		A	A	C	B	B	
		1 Req'd	1 Req'd	2 Req'd	2 Req'd	1 Req'd	1 Req'd	2 Req'd			2 Req'd
1942 T214	AMBULANCE Up to 81632103	922360	922361	921201	320771	916118	916119	921039	☆	☆	320771
1942 T214	AMBULANCE After 81632103	927428	927429	927340	☆	928656	928657	928660	927348	927348	☆

Below: The longer exhaust pipe was near the rear wheel.

Right: Set of leaf springs, specific to the WC54, without its protective envelope (a strapping part is missing) Note that the spring leaves have a single flange. Note also the cloth envelope for the leaves and the steel envelope to protect them.

Below, from left:
- Greasing the leaves.
- Greased paper protecting the leaves.
- Putting it all back by sliding the upper parts of the envelope over the leaves.
- Re-assembled unit including a re-made part because the original was missing.

Right: Steel "omega" used as a stop for the front leaf springs.

Below: Set of leaf springs specific to the ambulance, specially wrapped in grease.

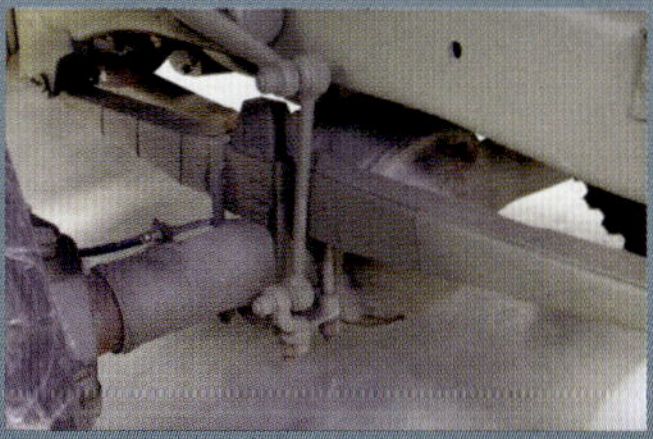

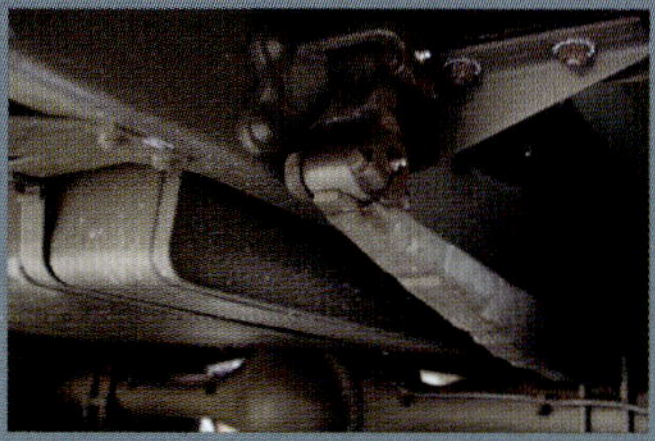

Ambulances and medical personnel on Guam, Mariana Islands. (*USAF*)

Above: Ambulance on Saipan. (*US Army*)

Left: Ambulance with trailer on a Ninth Air Force airstrip in Villaroche. (*USAF*)

2 Bodywork

The list of parts in Standard Nomenclature List (SNL) G657 dating back to World War II included the following bodywork suppliers:

- American Coach and Body Co., Cleveland, Ohio—emergency bodywork repairs WC60.
- Edward G. Budd Mfg. Co., Detroit, Michigan—reconnaissance and cargo bodywork.
- Gar Wood Industries, Detroit, Michigan—dump trucks.
- Highwood Trailer Co., Edgerton, Wisconsin—telephone installation bodywork.
- Proctor-Keefe Body Co., Detroit Michigan—Carryall bodywork.
- Wayne Works, Richmond, Indiana—ambulance bodywork.

The specific chassis for the Dodge WC54 was built in the Detroit factory, Michigan. Wayne Works at Richmond, Indiana, built the bodywork for the Dodge T214 WC54. The bodies were then delivered to the Dodge assembly lines.

Wayne Works was an American manufacturer making buses and other vehicles under the brand "Wayne." In the mid-20th century, Wayne was one of the main school bus producers in North America

Among the innovations the company introduced was the first use of the van chassis for a school bus and an improvement in the structural soundness of bus coachwork, using longitudinal panels to reduce body movement.

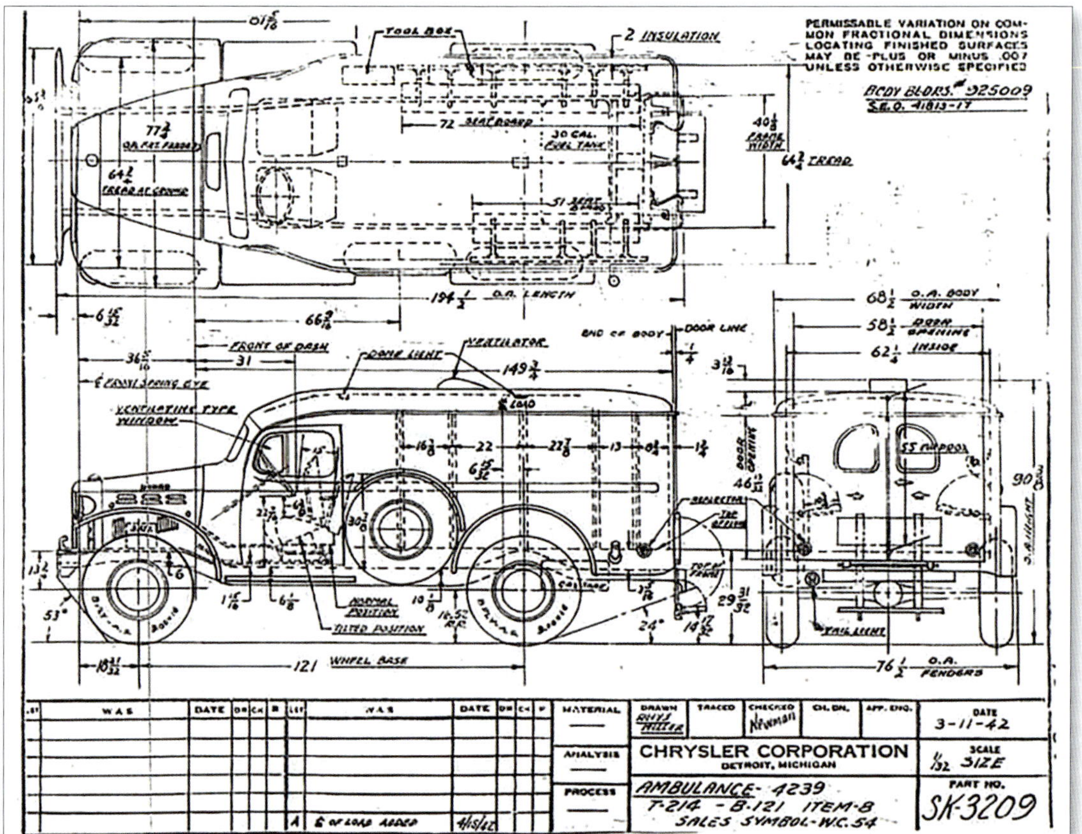

Right: Blueprint for WC54 bodywork.

Opposite: SNL G657—price list of Wayne Works part references for the ambulance body.

Parts listed on this page are serviced by and should be ordered from
Wayne Works, Richmond, Indiana

PRICE LIST

Part No.	Price
D4300	$ .20
D5077S	5.25
E6442—62"	.26
E6442—63½"	.27
E6442—99¼"	.40
E6443—62"	.37
E6443—63½"	.37
E6443—99¼"	.57
B6446A	.17
7342	45.53
7343	12.35
7345	1.83
7347—21"	.57
7347—31"	.85
7351	.98
7353	.70
7359A	2.76
7496A	5.25
7500	6.30
7508	.69
509	.70
510A	16.70
511A	24.75
517	11.70
518	11.70
26	3.27
30A	.35
56	.75
57	.74
60	.41
3	4.05
6	6.22
2	2.79
[illegible]	4.40
[illegible]	2.75
[illegible]	1.01
A	.10
[illegible]	.55
[illegible]	.03
[illegible]	.35
[illegible]	4.58
[illegible]	2.63
7690 .24,	.24
[illegible]	.86
[illegible]	.24
7695	$ .86
7697	.11
7701	1.15
7702	.22
7703	.26
7706A	21.60
7707A	17.34
7708	.86
7709	.86
7710	.79
7711	.29
7720	.07
7721—5"	.08
7721—6"	.09
7721—18¾"	.13
7721—28¼"	.16
7721—39¼"	.20
7724A	1.93
7731	10.38
7732	6.54
7734	35.10
7741	.15
7742A	15.60
7743A	15.60
7745	.45
7751A	5.18
7763	.13
7764	.16
7765A	.26
7766A	.26
7768A	2.79
7772	.08
7776	.70
7783	.23
7785	.67
7790	.32
7791	.34
7823	.43
7833A	7.60
7834A	2.59
7838A	.86
7842	.19
7843	.20
7844	3.10
7849	.15
7858	$ 1.69
7859	1.69
7860	31.60
7861	2.63
7862	2.63
7895	.20
7896	.22
7897	1.03
7898A	16.62
7899A	25.35
9025	.22
9029A	28.45
9030A	34.78
9038A	22.18
9039A	19.04
9044A	5.56
9046	3.34
9047	3.34
9193	2.17
9194	2.50
9195	.49
9196	.49
K9200	1.70
9275	.23
9299A	2.59
9447	16.30
9448	Sq. Yd. 6.25
9449	Sq. Yd. 6.25
9515	.10
9522A	27.37
9523A	39.72
9574A	9.62
9588	.70
9593	.40
9594	.40
9600A	14.98
9601A	10.18
9602	4.59
9603	3.67
9605	3.28
9614	10.90
9615	11.20
9624A	49.93
9630A	1.40
9651A	.70
9652A	.70
9654	$ .47
9659	.37
9660	1.02
9663A	7.40
9666A	9.59
9671A	1.39
9676—39"	.43
9676—47½"	.52
9676—52½"	.56
9676—53½"	.58
9676—58½"	.64
9676—64½"	.70
9682A	5.10
9683A	43.20
9684A	43.20
9691A	7.88
9712	4.73
9996	.65
9998	1.93
10006A	44.54
E10122A	.95
E10125	.71
E10127	.07
10273A	4.25
10274A	3.08
10448	.23
10453	.24
10454	.24
11019	.05
11042	.19
11043	.03
11144	6.98
11145	5.40
11185	2.18
11191	3.47
11334A	1.41
11347A	3.18
11348	1.25
11349	1.25
11355	16.20
11411	.40
11427A	3.15
11429	2.66
11430	2.66
11453A	.32
11454A	.32

major complete welded assemblies such as roofs, sides, floor and body parts not listed herein, order by description and model.

Also give the number shown in WAYNE WORKS name plate located inside above windshield.

The ambulance body was made of steel and the interior panels were made of Masonite called "Isorel." A thick band of cardboard was fitted between the body and the panels as insulation.

Two benches, folding down lengthways, were available for seven walking wounded. The rings and the supports mounted on the roof could take two shoulder-high stretchers. When the rear benches were folded up, two further stretchers could be placed on the floor. An extractor fan on the ceiling ventilated the rear compartment. The spare wheel was recessed in the rear compartment just behind the door on the driver's side.

During the war, Wayne Works also built mobile machining workshops, military buses, and semi-trailers used for transporting war workers; some models could carry up to 150 passengers.

Wayne Works references

Wayne bodyworks had their own references, different to Chrysler's. They consisted of four to five figures, sometimes with a letter.

Attaching the body to the chassis

The body was fixed to the chassis at 14 different points:

- Twelve screws (CC966555) resting on round rubber washers (CC890241).
- Two screws (CC966523) went through the floor, resting on wooden chocks with rubber pads (CC903097).

The wooden chocks were each fastened to the body by two wood screws with rounded heads. These kept the chocks in place when the bodywork was transported. Between the body and the chassis were placed 10 round rubber pads (CC930572), clipped to the body to ensure it was wedged.

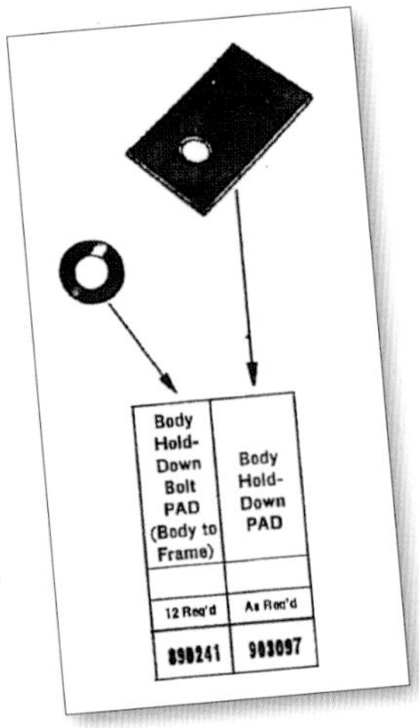

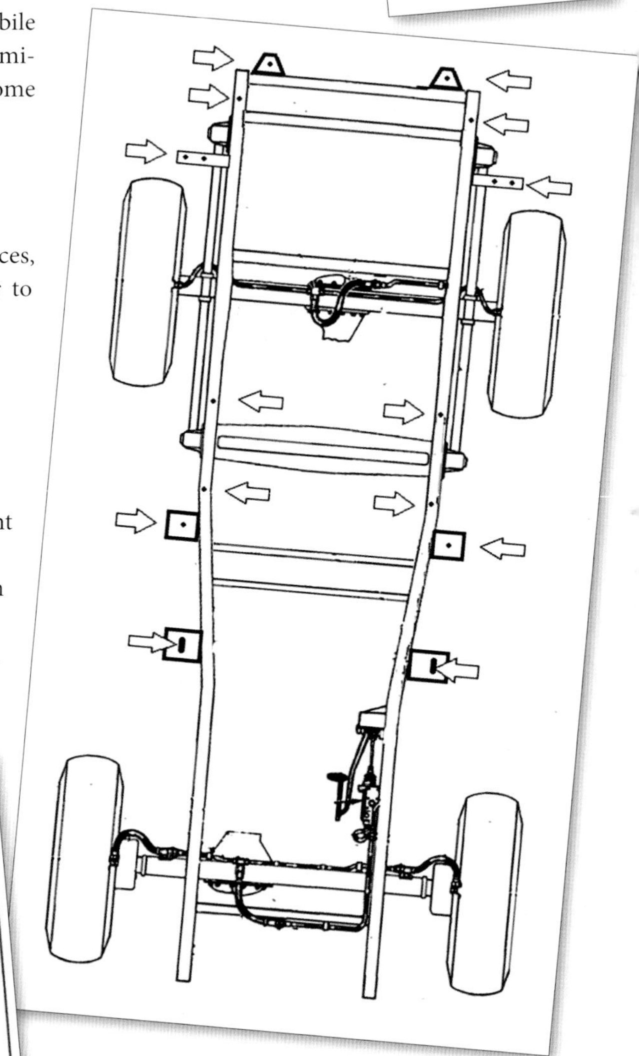

Part No.	PART NAME	Model Codes 4239
	GROUP 1807 BODY PARTS	
	BODY HOLD-DOWN PARTS	
	BODY HOLD-DOWN BOLT	
■844757	Bolt (1/2 - 20 x 3 3/4)	2
966553	Bolt.	12
▼120371	Nut (1/2 - 20)	12
▼178596	Lockwasher (1/2)	4
▼120392	Plainwasher (1/4)	2
■890241	Pad (body to frame) (2" dia. with 7/16" hole)	10
930572	Pad (body to frame)(2" diameter with clip)	10

Top: Adjusting chocks for the 14 attachment points on the body.

Above: Diagram showing the body attachment points.

Left: The list of elements attaching the body to the chassis.

Above: Chocks mounted on a vehicle which has not been disassembled since it was last rebuilt in 1945.

Above right: Original disassembled front body chocks from a 1943 WC54.

Right: Two screws with rounded heads hold the wooden chock between the body and the chassis.

Below: Rubber pad, reference CC930572.

Bottom left: The sheet metal used was 0.0394 in (1 mm) thick.

Bottom center and right: These dimensions are closer to the French norms than the American ones.

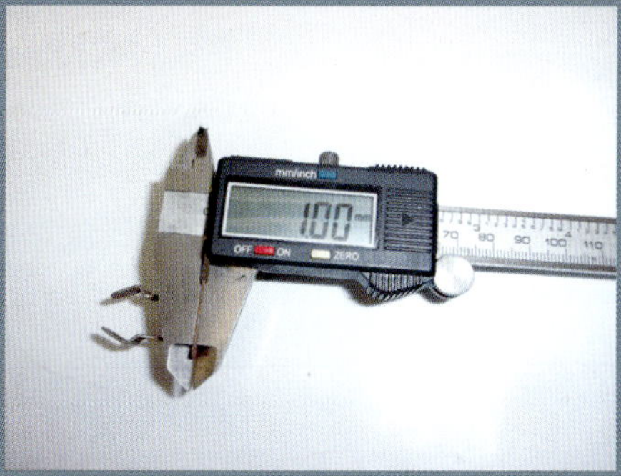

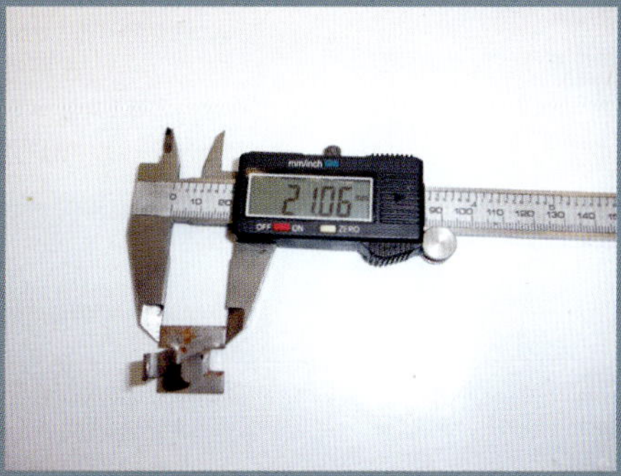

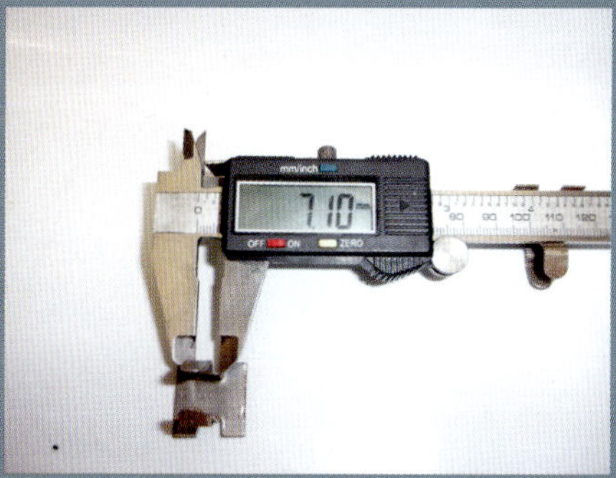

There was a type of felt pad held in place by a steel clip. This replaced the rubber pad when the French Army rebuilt the ambulances. The clip was made of 1-mm-thick sheet metal, whereas the American sheet steel standards were 0.036 in (0.91 mm) or 0.48 in (1.21 mm).

Interior: The Cab

Steering wheel

The steering wheel was made of black Bakelite on the early models. This became a green Bakelite from chassis 81552579 to 81550000. It is not known when the model with metal spokes was introduced.

Instrument panel/dashboard

The ambulance's instrument panel was fitted with the usual U.S. Army vehicle instruments.

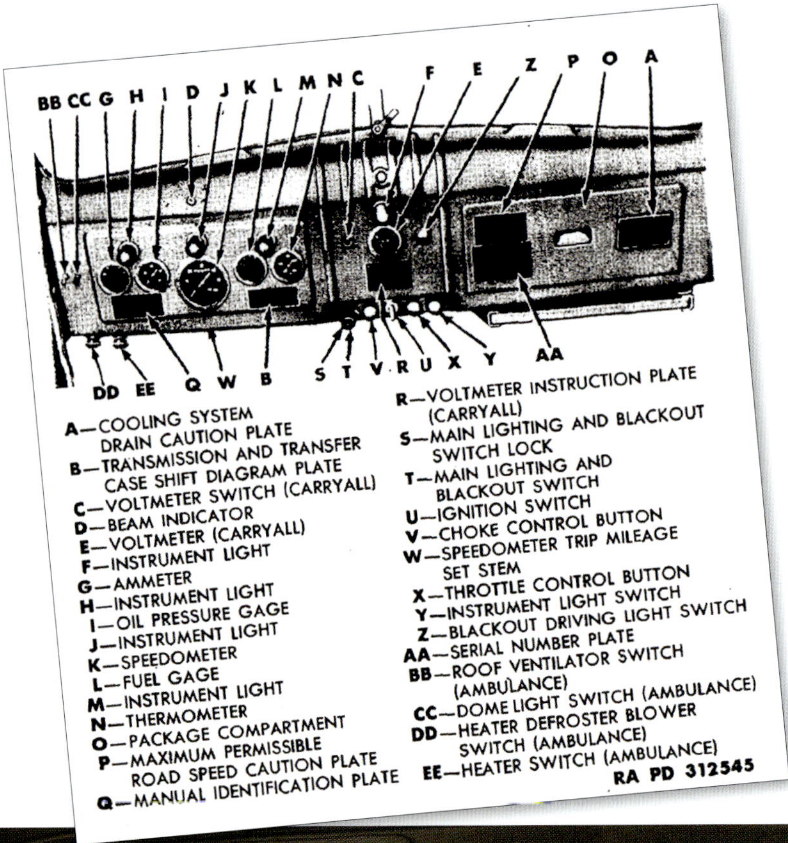

Right: Details of the dashboard. Note that C, E, F and R refer to the Carryall.

Below: View of the driver's position.

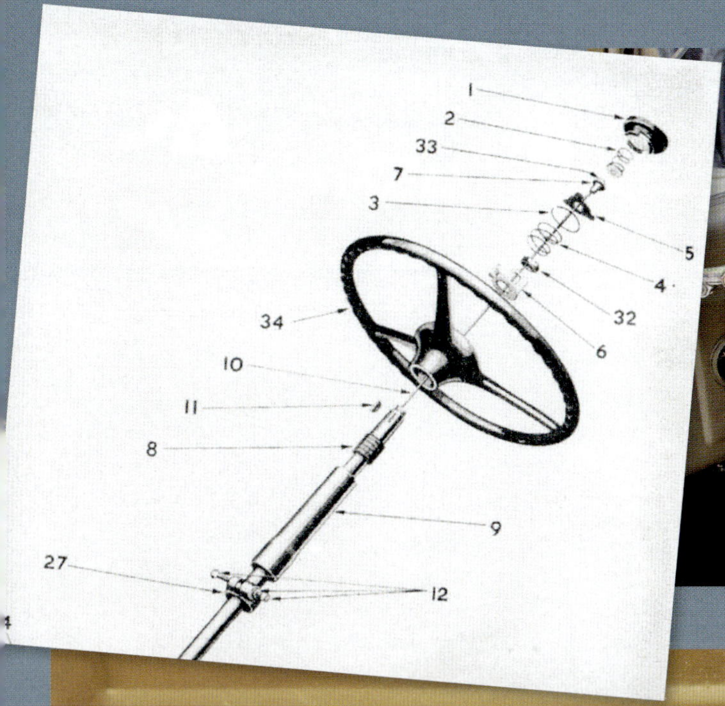

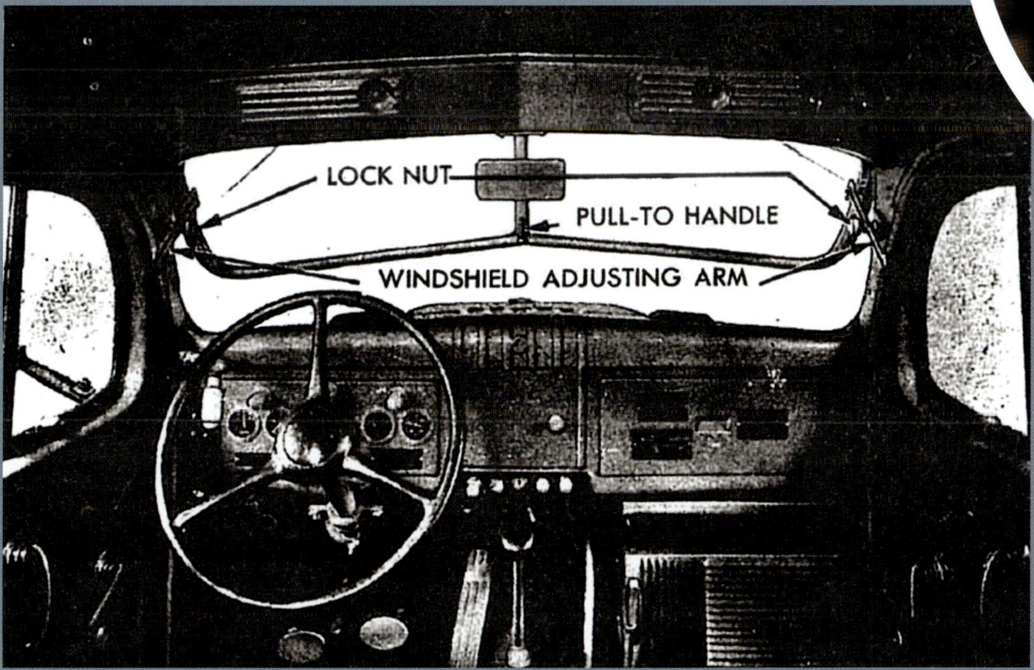

Top left: First type of steering wheel.

Top right: Third type of steering wheel with metal spokes.

Above left: Details of the central dashboard controls.

Above: Standard pull-out switch with its original label showing the different positions for use.

Left: Inside view of the driver's position with windshield components annotated.

Besides heating, also included were defrosting, inside lighting and rear section ventilation controls.

From left to right:

- Ammeter
- Oil pressure gauge
- Speedometer in miles per hour
- Fuel gauge
- Temperature gauge

The controls located to the right of the driver's position, in the center of the dash, are, from left to right (see page 19):

- Light switch
- Choke pullout stopper
- Ignition switch
- Manual throttle control
- Panel lights switch. The blackout (B/O) control was located on the central flat panel above the panel lights switch.

Controls specific to the ambulance are dealt with later.

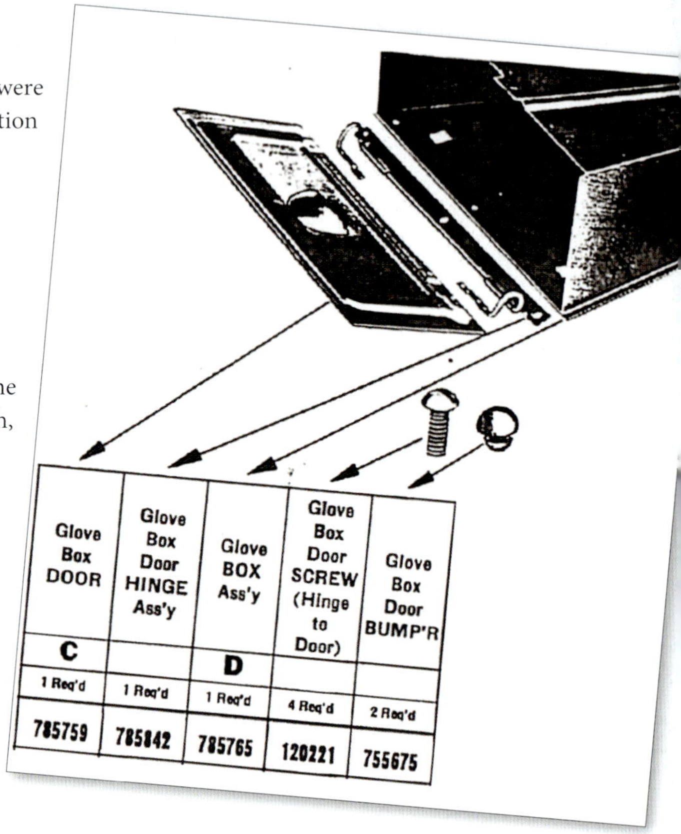

Above: Details of the elements making up the glovebox. There are four attachment screws for the glovebox door that are part of the door-hinge.

Below: The ammeter measured from -60/0/+60, a characteristic of Dodges. The TM9-808 publications plate is below.

Below right: Instrument arrangement on the dashboard.

Glovebox lid

The U.S. model consisted of two pieces of sheet metal folded by stamping (CC785759). The French model was simply made of mechanically welded sheet metal.

Closing the panel was dampened by two rubber pads (CC755675). It was held closed by two flat sheet metal springs (CC785913) specific to this glovebox.

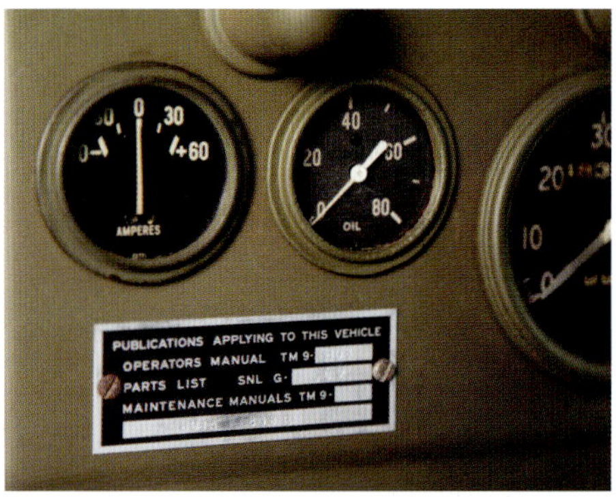

Right: Postwar glovebox lid. The holes were drilled later, this one being originally delivered without any holes.

Far right: The inside of the U.S. model of glovebox lid.

Below: Note the maker's plate ("Wayne Works") above the windshield. The crew has added "U.S." as well as the name of a crew member ("PFC Nekas") on the windshield. (*US Signals*)

Instruction and identification plates

There were five instruction and identification plates located as follows:

From left to right:

- The instruction manual numbers applying to the vehicle: "PUBLICATIONS APPLYING TO THIS VEHICLE"
- The instruction plate for the gear and transfer box levers: "DISENGAGE FRONT AXLE DRIVE WHEN..."

On the glovebox:

- Gear speeds (top left): "CAUTION MAX. PERMISSIBLE ROAD SPEEDS"
- Vehicle identification details (bottom left): "DODGE TRUCKS"
- Cooling system directions (right): "DRAINING COOLING SYSTEM"

The CC615808 part reference included the five plates.

To the top right (interior, looking out) of the passenger-side windshield wiper motor was displayed the plate of the bodywork's maker: "THE WAYNE WORKS."

Each bodywork model had a model number followed by a series number. These were identified on an oval plate made of aluminum alloy. The body model number of the ambulance was 4239. The plate was located on the bottom of the front right-hand door post; it was attached by two flat sheet metal screws.

Identification plate

This was shown in TM9 808; other models appeared at the end of the war (and postwar for the reconstructions).

The first vehicles were delivered by the Quartermaster Corps (QMC); this was indicated on the plate in the "SUPPLY ARM" area (see plate on page 23).

Below: Bodywork maker plate: "B-147" is the same for the WC54 series; the figure "42" is thought to be the year of construction.

Bottom: The glovebox lid with its instruction and identification plates.

Above: Where the bodywork plate is located. This image has been rotated 90 degrees. The ground is to the right.

Above right: Bodywork number plate showing the ambulance model number "4239" and the individual body number.

Right: Identification plate with the two types of inscriptions possible for the "SUPPLY ARM." The "ORDNANCE DEPT" stamp appeared in mid-1942.

Below right: A publications plate. This version appeared in mid-1942.

Bottom: An example of glovebox plates affixed to a reconstructed ambulance. In this case, it has been assigned to a reconstructed Dodge WC54. The date is stamped on the reconstruction plate (May 1953).

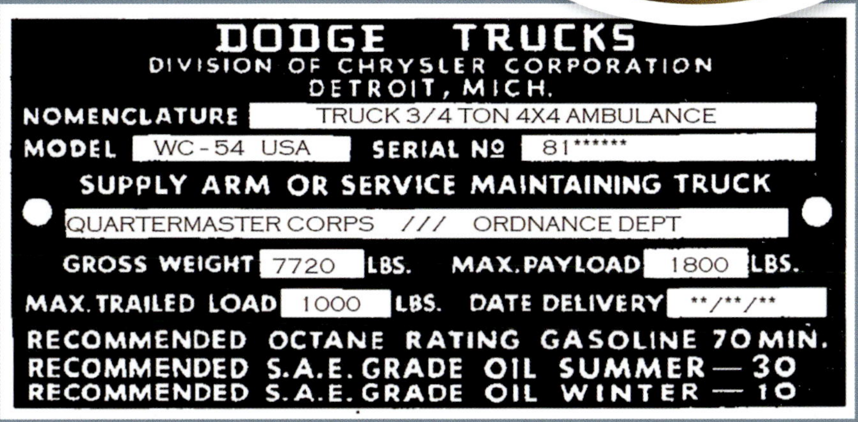

Because the vehicle service was reorganized, the QMC transferred its management to the Ordnance Department. This transfer was effective from mid-July and the beginning of August 1942; "ORDNANCE DEPT" was stamped in place of "QUARTERMASTER CORPS." This modification implied the publication plates were also changed in the maintenance manuals. The publications coming from the QMC were from the series TM10, and those from the Ordnance Department were from the series TM9. This modification also appeared in the summer of 1942.

Map table

The map table was located below the glovebox. It slid in and out on two rails.

There were two map table models:

The first, CC966702, was a simple wooden rectangle 14.06 x 13.86 inches. It was 0.7480 inches thick and had two notches on the side that engaged the lugs of the rails. A small recess under the front of the table helped with handling.

The second model, CC918831, was recognizable by an extra notch at the rear of the table. This enabled the speedometer cable to be slid along it. This second model was mounted from chassis 81625758 onwards, but also included 81625256 and 81625476–81625734.

Speedometer cable

The speedometer cable was 73 inches long (CC840460). On the first model of map table, the cable went through the firewall with the choke cable, the manual accelerator and the temperature probe. With the second model of map table, as mentioned above, the cable ran behind it and through the passenger floor.

Interior rear-view mirror

The interior rear-view mirror with its fastening tab can be found by referencing CC920680.

Cabin upholstery

The cabin uprights were equipped with compressed

An original example of the second wooden table version. The difference from the previous version is not visible when the table is in use.

Above: The interior rear-view mirror and the access panel for the driver's side windshield-wiper motor.

Right: The speedometer cable passing behind the map table.

Below: Cable mounting on the firewall for the choke, manual accelerator and the insulation of the temperature probe. The empty position on the left was for the speedometer cable on the first model.

cardboard fittings at each end of the windshield frame. Each fitting was held in place by four dished screws, as well as the extremity of the surrounding door trim which was turned back over it.

References: CC889072 for the right fitting and CC889074 for the left.

The inside frame on the cab door consisted of a band of canvas attached with twist pins. It was held in place by a ribbed trim which went round the frame. This assembly meant any gaps between the bodywork and the doors were draft proof.

Heat shield

The heat shield was specific to the WC54 ambulance because of the shape of its dashboard. It enabled the de-icing and heating attachments to be positioned. It was made up of a sheet of compressed cardboard and glued honeycombed cardboard and was held in place by 12 black clips (CC788361).

Front floor mat

The driving cab had a floor mat (CC966791) for its rear section. It covered the shape of the floor but left the front seat attachments visible.

An extension (CC991715) existed but it is not known what shape it was. Instructions for assembling a mat also described how to fit it. It was replaced by a central leather section (CC966650) but that was not available before chassis 81625758 (and 81625256) or for the series 81625476–81625734.

Installation instructions for floor mats

Place the rear section of the floor mat in position and install the screws with plain washers. Install the center and two end linoleum retainer angles. Work the front section of the floor mat into place so the openings in the mat will slide down over the gearshift, hand brake, transfer case levers, and accelerator pedal. Attach the accelerator pedal to the accelerator pedal rod. Install floor mat screws.

Position the driver's seat so it is raised to its highest position and install the cap screws with lock washers. Install the one short cap screw in the right rear screw hole of the seat adjusting mechanism. Place the attendant's seat in position in the cab and tilt it forward. Install the seat support bracket cap screws with lock washers.

Original unassembled heat wall.

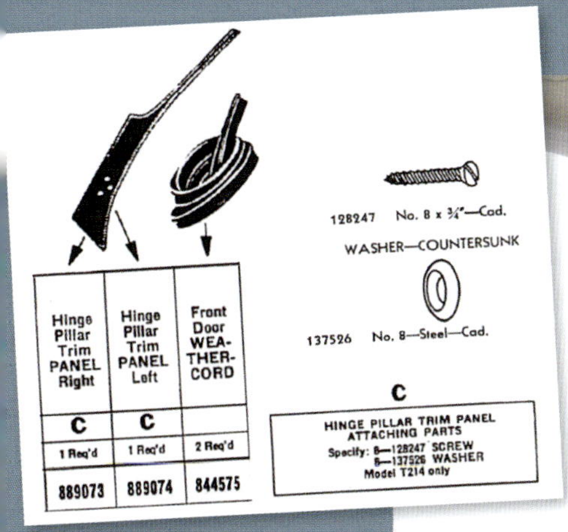

Hinge Pillar Trim PANEL Right	Hinge Pillar Trim PANEL Left	Front Door WEA-THER-CORD
C	C	
1 Req'd	1 Req'd	2 Req'd
889073	889074	844575

128247 No. 8 x ¾"—Cad.

WASHER—COUNTERSUNK

137526 No. 8—Steel—Cad.

C

HINGE PILLAR TRIM PANEL ATTACHING PARTS
Specify: 8—128247 SCREW
8—137526 WASHER
Model T214 only

Top left: Draft-proofing for the body upright and the inside door band.

Right: Draft-proofing on the body upright.

Far right: This is what is presumed to be the style of the front floor mat based upon the information known at present.

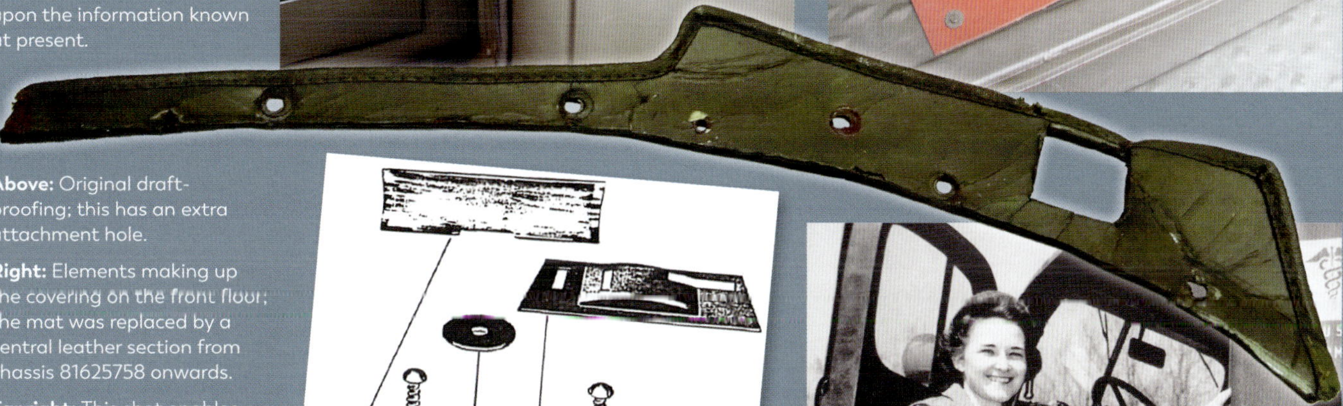

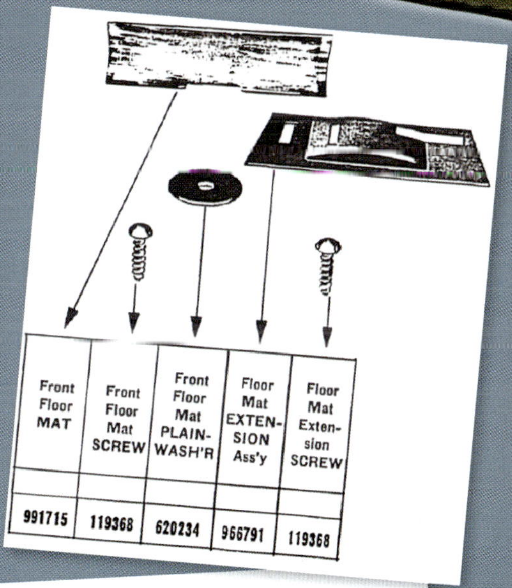

Front Floor MAT	Front Floor Mat SCREW	Front Floor Mat PLAIN-WASH'R	Floor Mat EXTEN-SION Ass'y	Floor Mat Exten-sion SCREW
991715	119368	620234	966791	119368

Above: Original draft-proofing; this has an extra attachment hole.

Right: Elements making up the covering on the front floor; the mat was replaced by a central leather section from chassis 81625758 onwards.

Far right: This shot enables us to see the mat lifting off the floor. The handle of the Appleton searchlight is visible just above the servicewoman's shoulder. (*US Army*)

Bottom: Notice explaining how to install the front floor mats (as per pages 26 and 28).

(10) Install Floor Mat (Ambulance Only). Place the rear section of the floor mat in position and install the screws with plain washers. Install the center and two end linoleum retainer angles. Work the front section of the floor mat into place so that the openings in the mat will slide down over the gearshift, hand brake, transfer case levers, and accelerator pedal. Attach the accelerator pedal to the accelerator pedal rod. Install floor mat screws. Position the driver's seat so that it is raised to its highest position and install the cap screws with lock washers. Install the one short cap screw in the right rear screw hole of the seat adjusting mechanism. Place the attendant's seat in position in the cab and tilt it forward. Install the seat support bracket cap screws with lock washers.

Above: Oran, Algeria, June 1944. This shot, taken from a documentary, shows the gusset on the front seats as well as their rounded backs. (*Critical Past, Licence 65685030843*)

Bottom left: Driver's side

Bottom right: Passenger side.

Front seats

The front seats, 9683A (left) and 9684A (right), were adapted to the driver's cab in the ambulance. They were distinguished by their floor attachments. The driver's seat was fixed to a mounting on rails so it could be moved backwards and forwards; it could also be tipped. Both seats were designed with a brown fake leather cover.

There was only one style of seat; it had a very rounded back. The squarer models were produced after the war. There are stories of seat covers but no documentation mentions them. They could be a postwar modification or a special production.

Below: References for the driver's seat, and its mechanism, and the passenger seat; the references show this model of seat was specific to the WC54.

YEAR AND ENGINEERING SYMBOL	Drivers SEAT Assembly		Attend. SEAT Ass'y	
	Com-plete	Less Adjust-ing Mech-anism	With Bracket, AngleLeg, Yoke Pin &Seat Leg Att. Angle	Less Support and Attach-ing Leg
	1 Req'd	1 Req'd	1 Req'd	1 Req'd
1941—T207	⊠	⊠	⊠	⊠
1941—T211	⊠	⊠	⊠	⊠
1941—T215	⊠	⊠	⊠	⊠
1942—T214	9624A	9683A	10006A	9684A

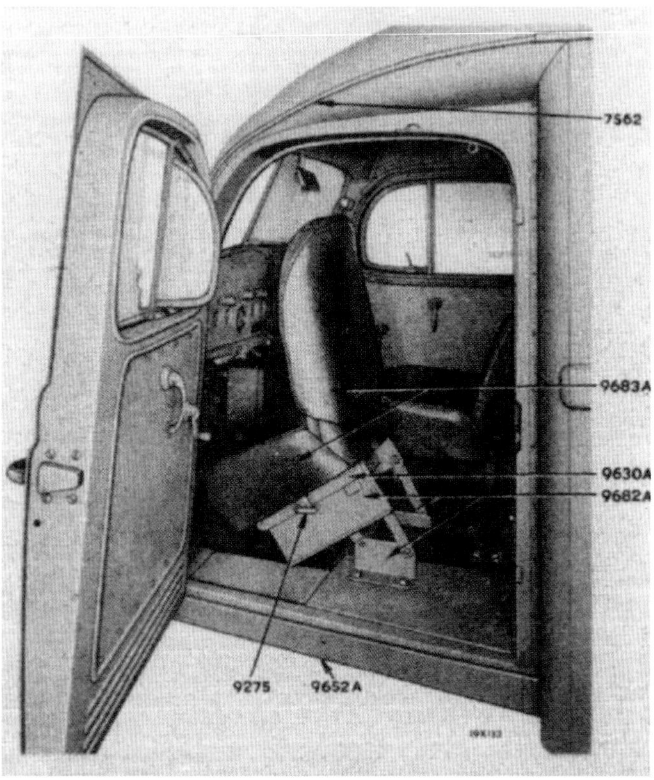

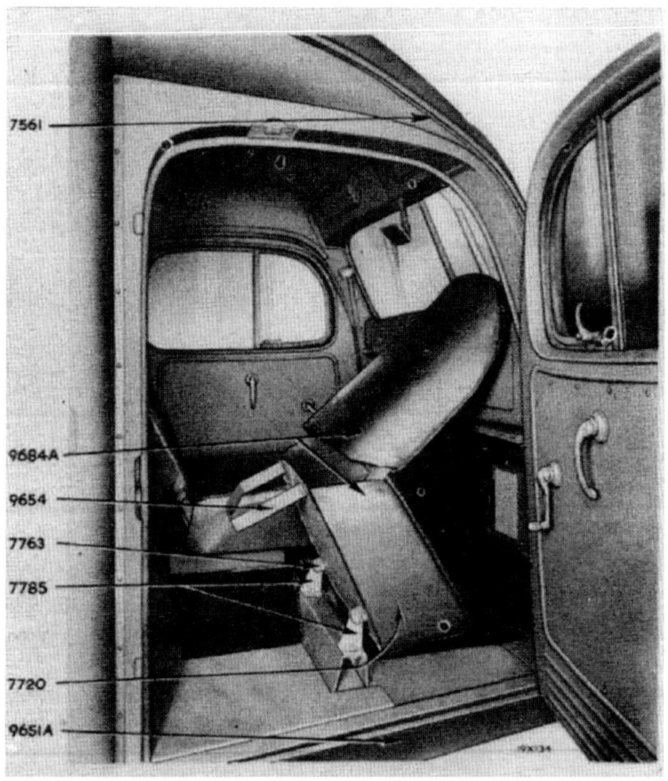

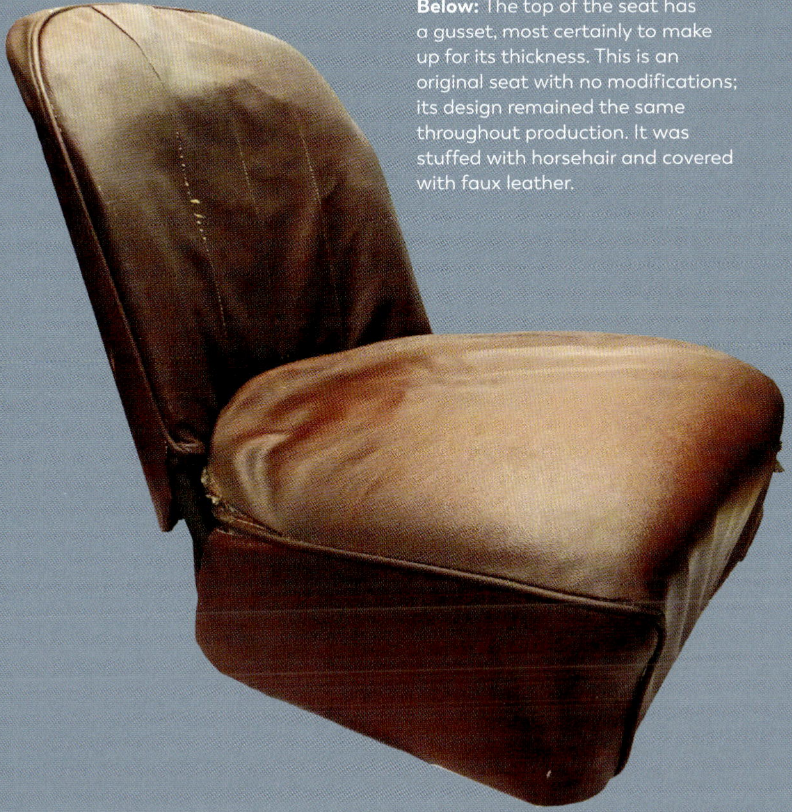

Below: The top of the seat has a gusset, most certainly to make up for its thickness. This is an original seat with no modifications; its design remained the same throughout production. It was stuffed with horsehair and covered with faux leather.

Above: The top of the seat had a gusset enabling it to "follow" when squashed as somebody sat down.

Below: Tipping mechanism for the driver's seat. It could be adjusted from front to rear in three positions.

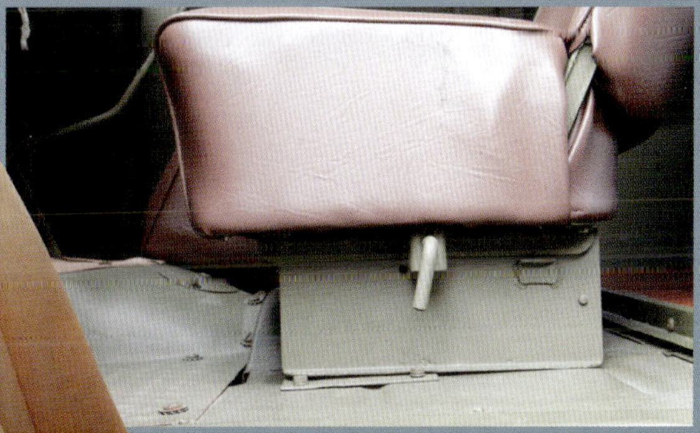

Bottom: A French-made seat, the screws and inserts were metric.

Inside: The body

Rear floor mats

The rear floor was covered with thick red-brown linoleum (Wayne Works reference 11355). The size of the floor mat on the WC54, reference 9447, according to the 1942 G502 catalogue, was 47 3/8 inches wide by 102 inches long. The width between the WC27's sides was 62¼ inches, the same as the WC54. The floor under the storage boxes was thus partly covered with linoleum.

This floor mat was held in place by the boxes, the rear bodywork traverse, and three retainers at the front—a central one and two retaining brackets. The brackets were located behind the front seats and were identified by 11453A for the right-hand one and 11454A for the left-hand one. The central retention was 11411. These three front elements also held the front floor mat in place because they were S-shaped.

Fuel transmitter panel

Above the fuel tank on the floor is a piece of round sheet metal (9515) held in place by three screws. This panel covered the access to the fuel tank level transmitter.

Body color

The inside color of the rear body was entirely olive drab and painted this color in the factory. Some were painted white and appeared in the middle of 1945. This was a modification especially for the dental services. The ambulance was then no longer used in its original form. This modification was mainly carried out in Asia. Modifying the WC54 for other tasks started from 1945 onwards. The end of the war in Europe reduced the need for emergency vehicles. Finally, the WC64KD ambulance appeared and replaced the WC54.

It is possible there were color changes for some vehicles assigned to the AFS (American Field Services).

These were modifications carried out in the field and were absolutely exceptional. The inside of the body of the Dodge WC54s in the production series was never painted white. It appeared on the vehicles rebuilt by the Etablissements de Resérve Générale du Matériel (ERGM) of the French Army and on vehicles assigned to fire departments.

Below right: A French ambulance in Indochina. It is recognizable by its registration number "IC" (from 1946 to 1954). The interior of the body has been repainted cream-white.

Below: A detailed view of some of the accessories for the vehicle's rear body.

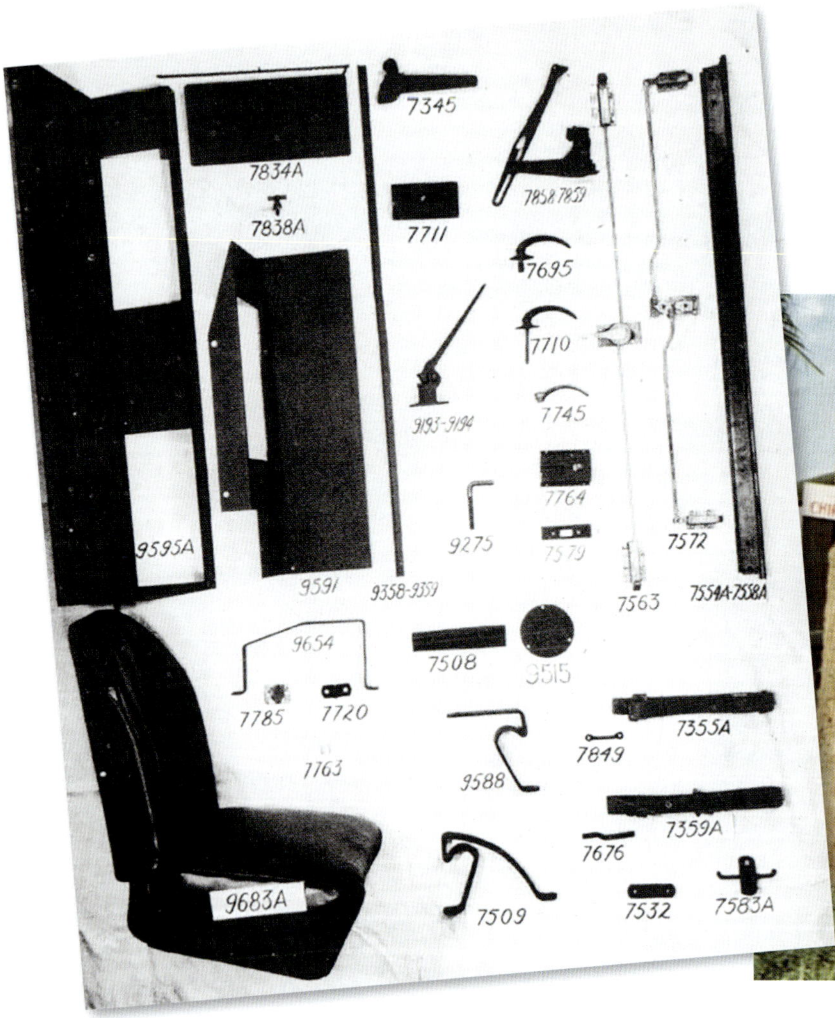

Above: View of the floor covered with linoleum

Top right: Access panel to the fuel transmitter.

Right: 35th General Hospital, Nadzab, New Guinea. (*National Library of Medicine*)

Below: 35th General Hospital, New Guinea. The dark interior indicates the inside of the body is painted the same as the outside. (*National Library of Medicine*)

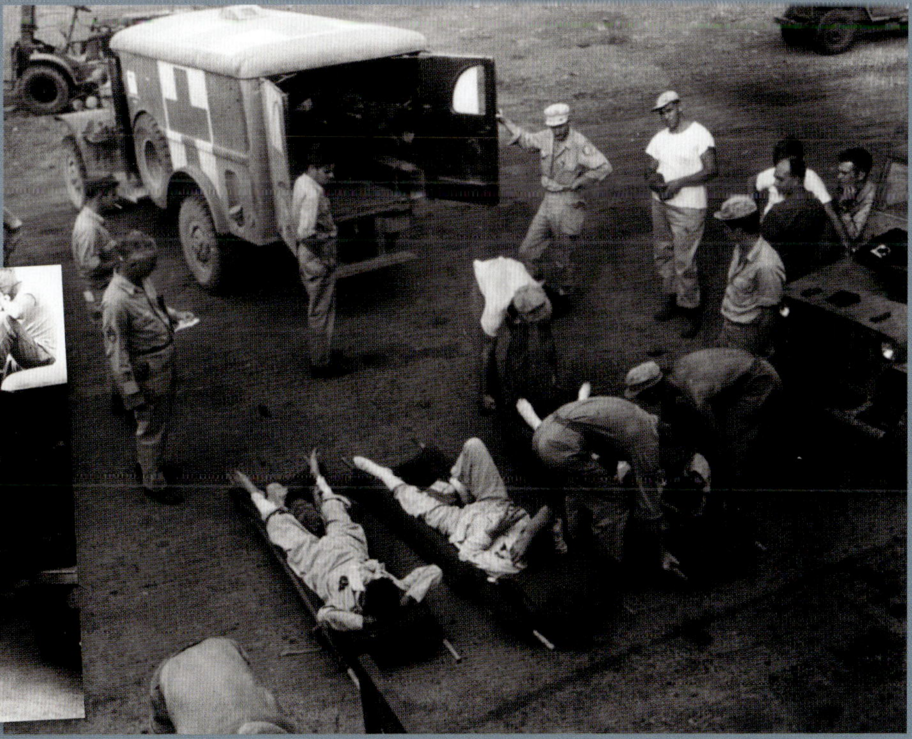

Interior side wall

The side panels of the body were not made of steel. They were a compressed cardboard called Masonite and attached by specific Phillips screws and washers inserted into the steel armatures of the bodywork.

All the surfaces except the floor were insulated with cardboard.

The bottoms of the walls between the outside and the inside were open, the insulation resting on an L-shaped angle iron.

Stretcher mountings

The stretcher supports are often missing or modified on unrestored vehicles. There were three 7509 supports, and a specific 9588 that took the location of the spare wheel into account. They were attached by two screws at the same height. Reinforcing them, by adding backing plates, was a later modification. There were two 7509 supports on the right and one on the left at the rear; the 9588 support was at the front on the left.

In order to get the stretcher to sit better on its supports, the brackets were covered by a leather sheath (7508).

Stretcher straps

The vehicle was equipped with four straps (11347A) which, in pairs, supported the stretcher in its open position. They were fitted with a hook which was attached to an oblong ring (7530A) solidly screwed into the ceiling armature of the bodywork.

Below: A stretcher held in position using the straps.

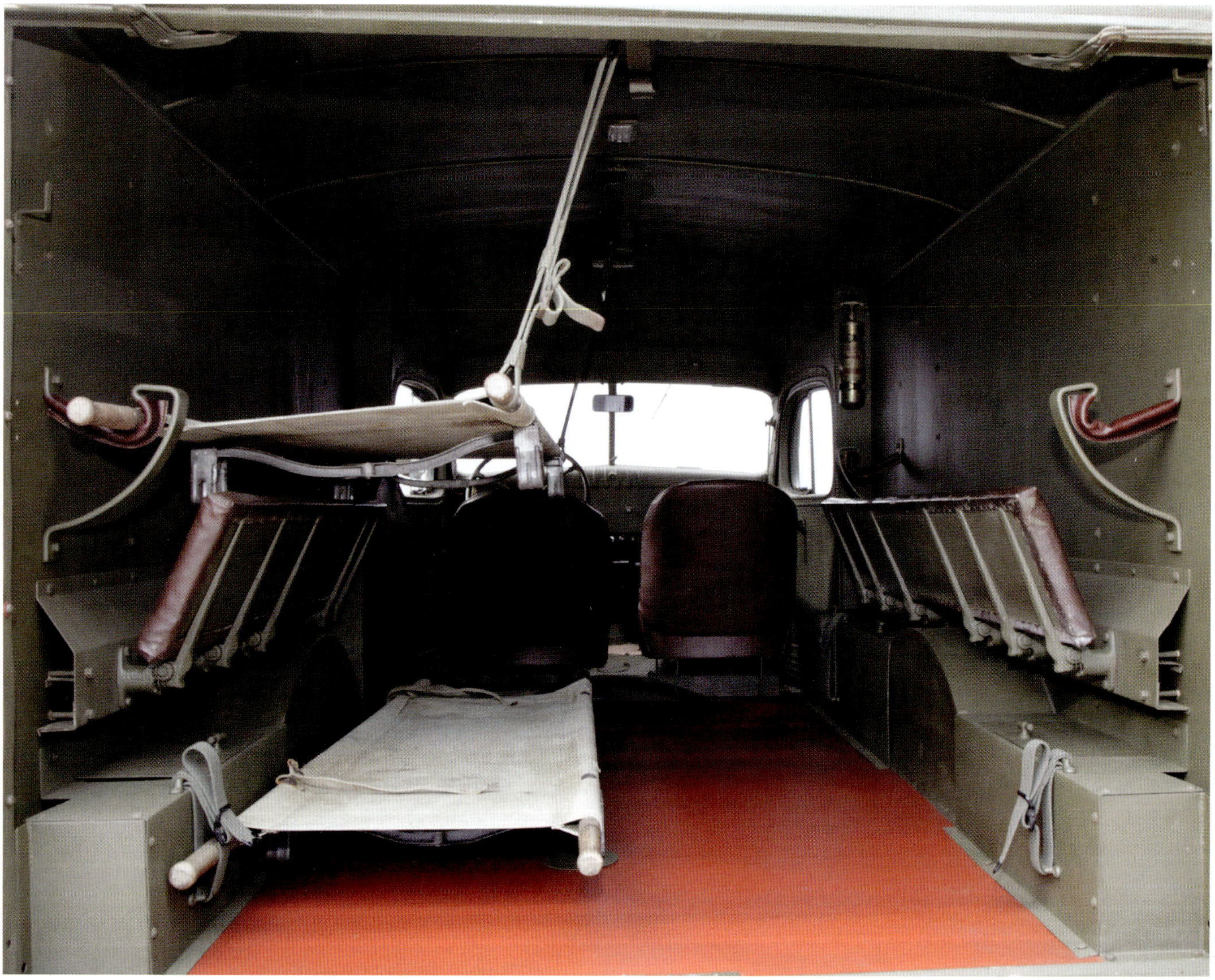

Above: Original cardboard insulation used to line the interior sides of the body and the ceiling.

Above center: This style of screw allowed the following elements to be attached: inside walls, the boxes to the floor, the edge of the sheet metal of the front ceiling, the rear floor traverse, and the three strips holding the floor mat in place behind the passenger seats. For fixing the walls, the screws were accompanied by a thin flat washer to increase the surface pressure applied to the panel.

Top: A screw and washer set holding the side wall in place.

Above right: Original brown leather sheath painted green and white.

Right and far right: Stretcher supports fastened to an upright on the wall, the four supports having the same type of leather sheath.

Below: This photo enables us to see the detail of the strap loops as well as their position when not in use. (*American Red Cross*)

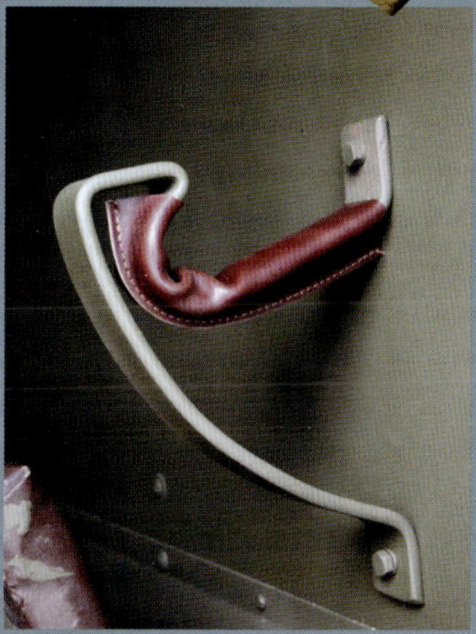

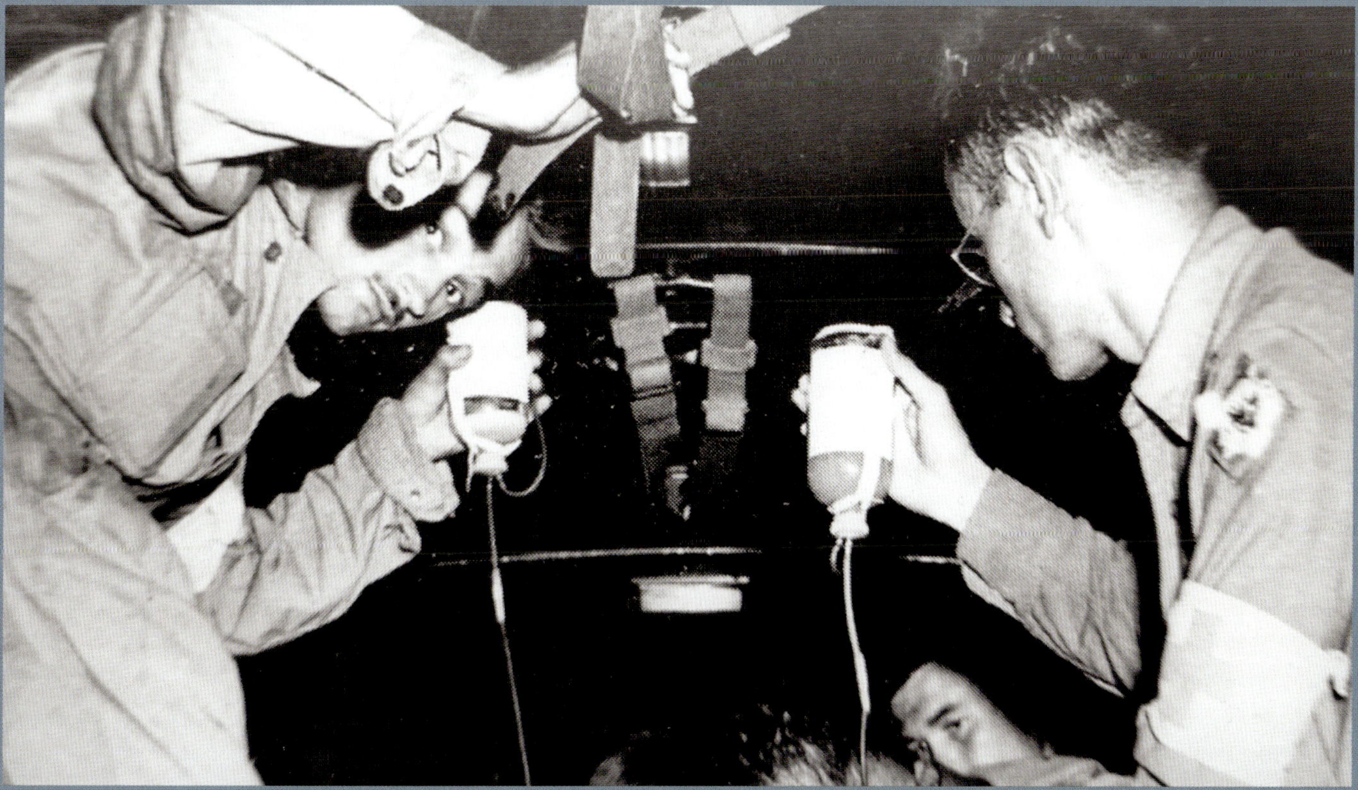

Stretcher strap supports

When the stretchers were not in use, they were laid flat against the ceiling with the help of the 7583A fitting.

Splint brackets

The 7676 bracket was for holding splinted limbs. The support fittings were reinforced behind the wall by a wooden backing plate. The left-hand support received arm splints with the right being for legs.

Ceiling trim

The ceiling trims joined the panels making up the interior ceiling of the body. There were six of them. They were made up of two elements: the first fixed the panel to the body with metal screws; the second covered the first, hiding the screw. These metal moldings were often replaced by wooden trim after the war.

Ceiling lights

The inside of the vehicle was lit by two E10122A ceiling lights. They were both switched on or off by a two-position switch (CC924079) located on the dashboard to the driver's left. This switch was to the right of the extractor fan switch.

The ceiling lights worked independently of the main lighting switch ("LIGHTS") used for the vehicle's exterior lights.

Below: Details of the length of the trim holding up the ceiling.

YEAR AND ENGINEERING SYMBOL	MOULDING Inside Trim 62"	RETAINER Moulding Trim 62"	MOULDING Inside 63½"	RETAINER Moulding Inside 63½"	MOULDING Inside 99¼"	RETAINER Moulding Inside 99¼"
	3 Req'd	3 Req'd	1 Req'd	1 Req'd	2 Req'd	2 Req'd
1942—T214	E-6442-62	E-6443-62	E-6442-63½	E-6443-63½	E-6442-99¼	E-6443-99¼

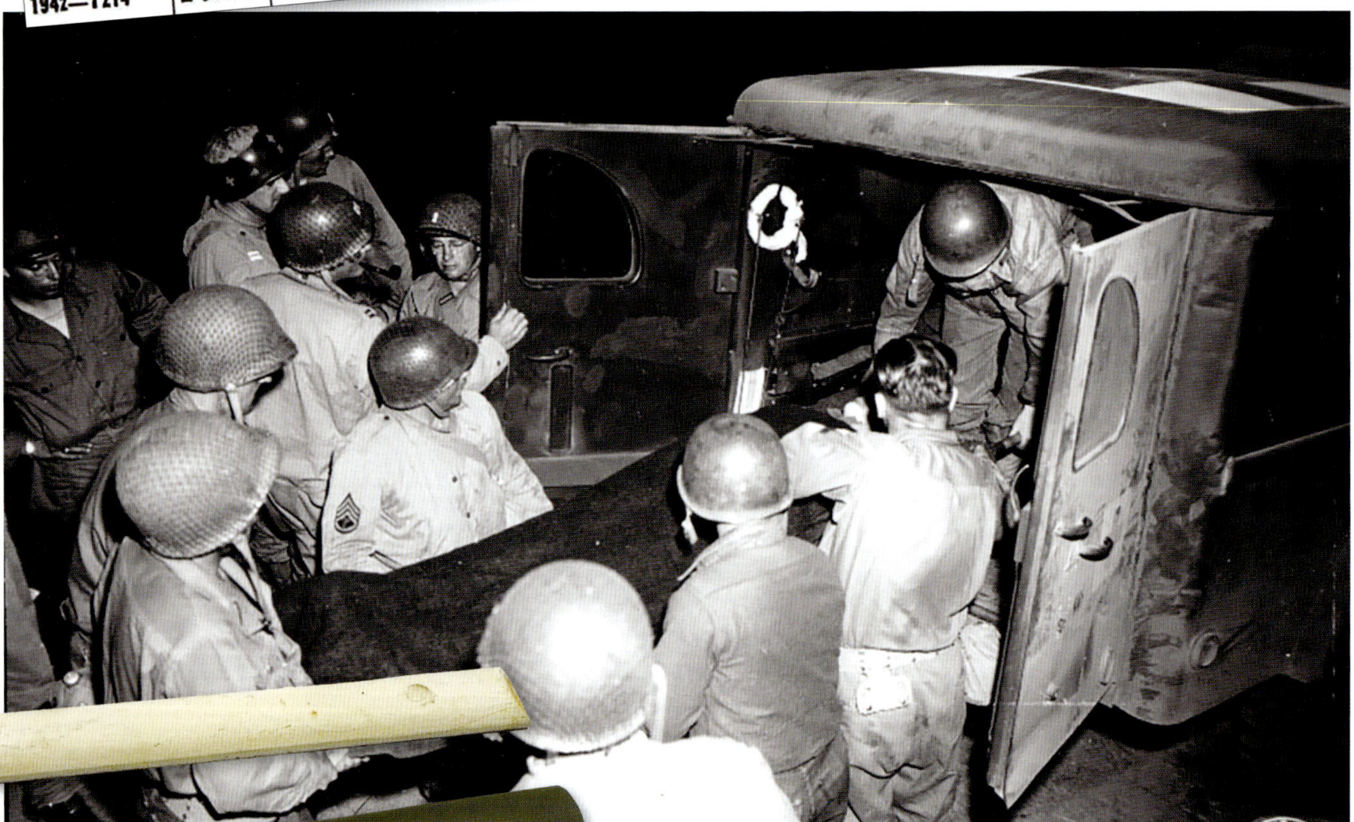

Below: Injured in a jeep accident during maneuvers, the patient is being transported by the medical services. This photo allows us to clearly see the placement for the splints. (*NARA*)

Inset: The white trim is made of wood; the French Army's ERGM used this to replace the original.

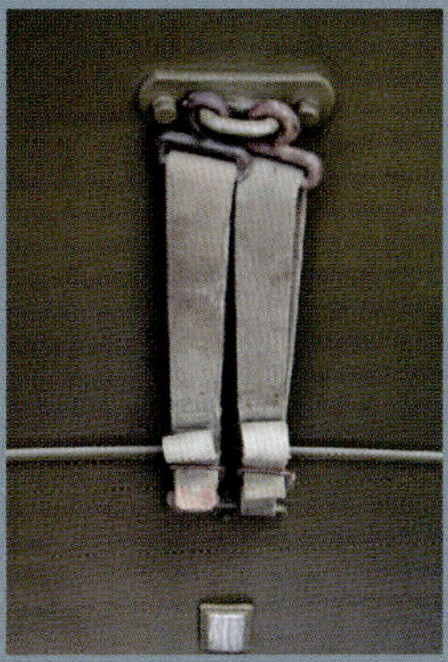
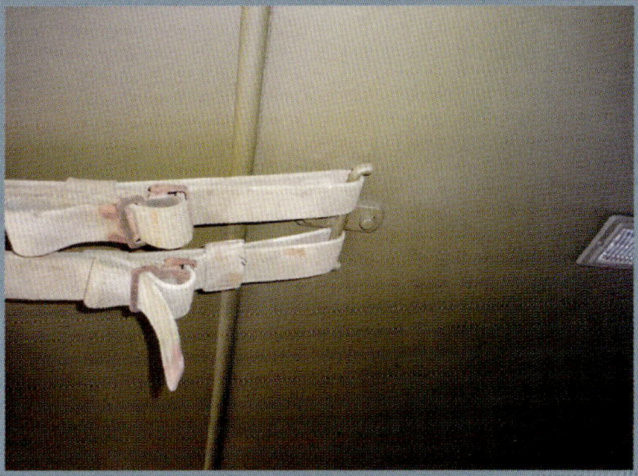

Above left: The stretcher straps were held flat to the ceiling when not in use.

Above center left: The plate (7530A) enabling the stretcher straps to be kept taut when not in use.

Above center right: The wooden reinforcement used to attach the hooks holding the splints.

Above right: Wooden reinforcement fitting with two nails, hidden under the hook which was positioned over it and attached by two wood screws.

Above left: The 7676 hook for holding arm splints.

Above right: The hook for holding leg splints.

Below: The trim hid the screws from sight; however, the second ceiling panel from the front had a series of screws without any trim. Indeed, this trim was only positioned on the sheet metal joins, at the rear end and on the sides.

Bottom: The forward ceiling was held in place by molded trim.

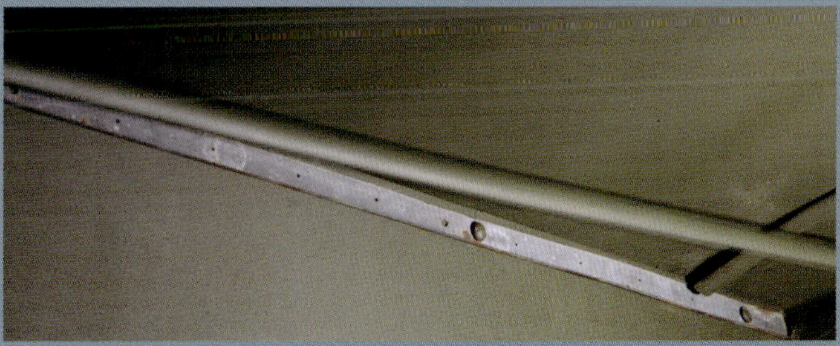

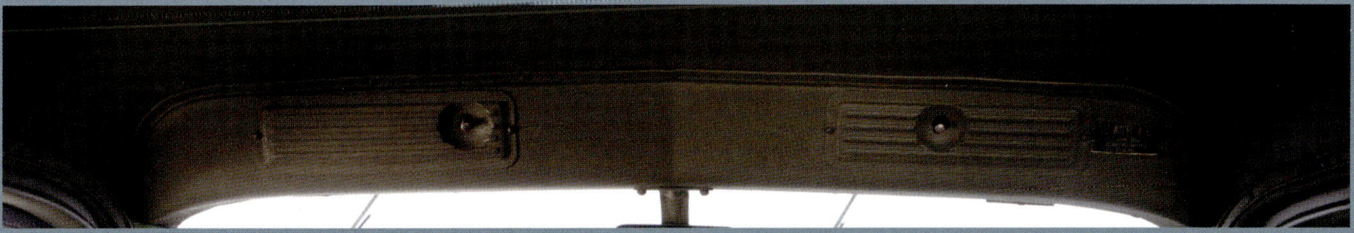

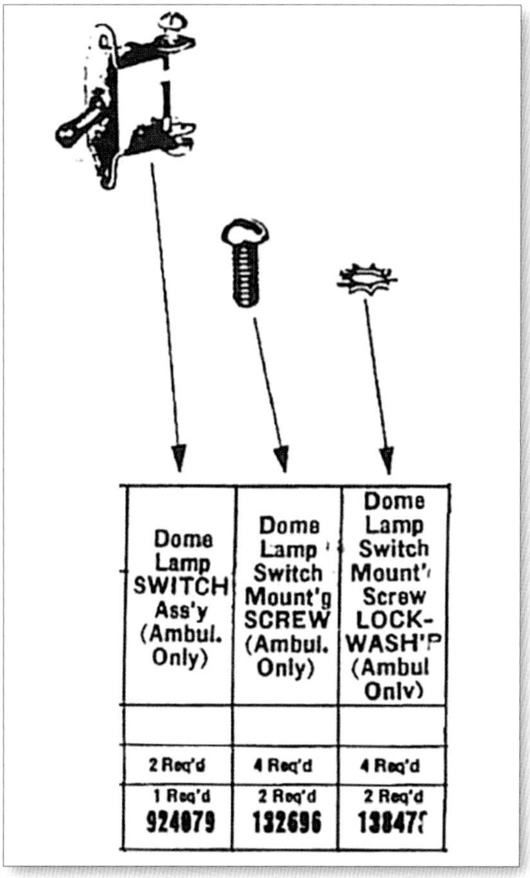

Dome Lamp SWITCH Ass'y (Ambul. Only)	Dome Lamp Switch Mount'g SCREW (Ambul. Only)	Dome Lamp Switch Mount'g Screw LOCK-WASH'R (Ambul Only)
2 Req'd	4 Req'd	4 Req'd
1 Req'd	2 Req'd	2 Req'd
924079	132696	13847?

Right: Switches for the ceiling light and extractor fan. There were two units fitted.

Below: This view of the roof shows the stamped form of the extractor fan dome; the first series of the 64KD was fitted with the previous model as fitted to the WC54. (*NARA*)

Extractor fan

The rear body had an air extractor on the ceiling. It consisted of a ventilator motor (7860), a protective grille to prevent the blades from being touched, and an adjustable air flow opening. On the outside, the extraction was protected by a dome welded to the roof. There was also a stamped version of the dome which was installed on the Dodge WC64KD.

The extractor fan was activated by the two-position switch (CC924079) located to the left of the light switch on the dashboard.

Rear benches

The benches were fitted to the wall by two rows of hexagonal screws on the lower part. Alternating semi-rounded and wood screws fixed the upper row into the wooden reinforcements nailed behind the panel.

The benches consisted of an oak plateau with filling made of a layer of cotton. The fabric covering the rear benches is a matter of disagreement because there is no reference as to what it was made of.

There were often two materials: faux brown leather, the same as that on the front seats; and olive drab cotton canvas. The pre-Dodge WC54 ambulances had covers made of canvas.

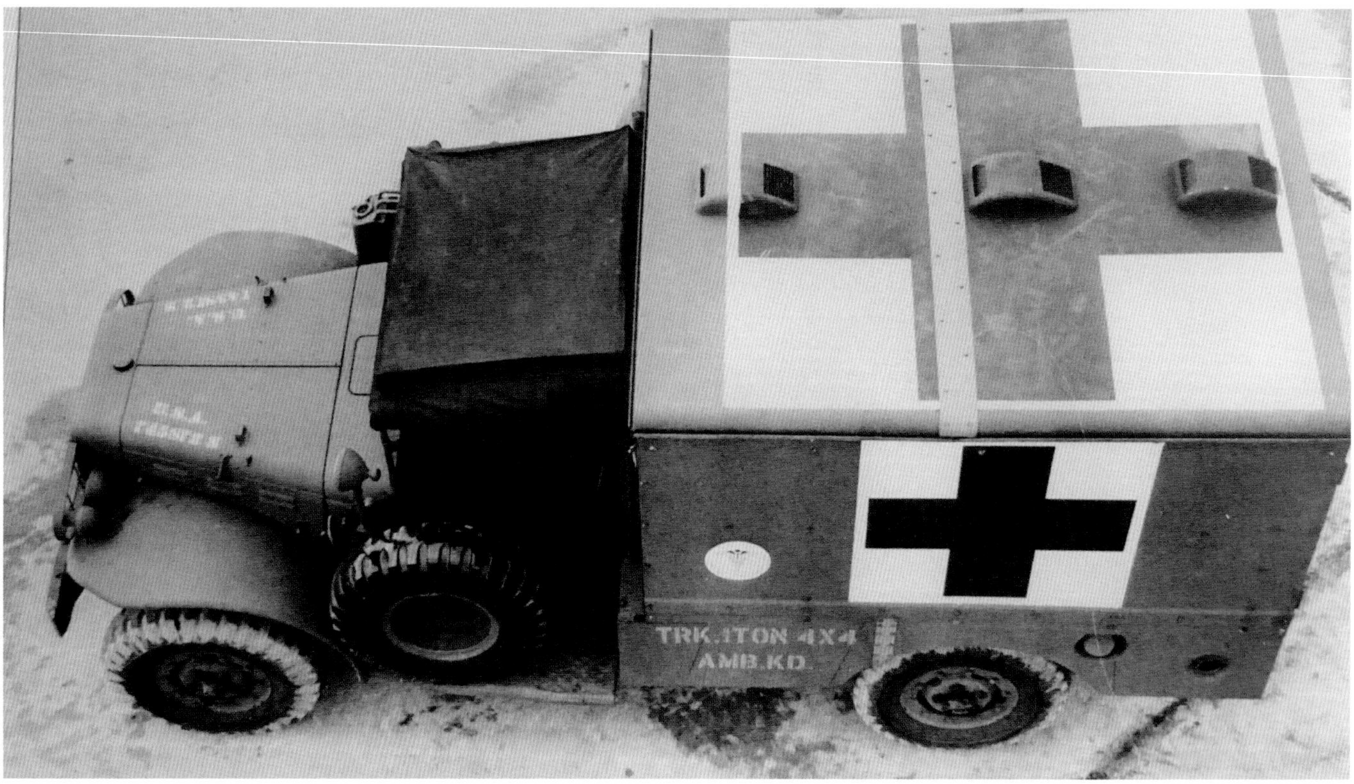

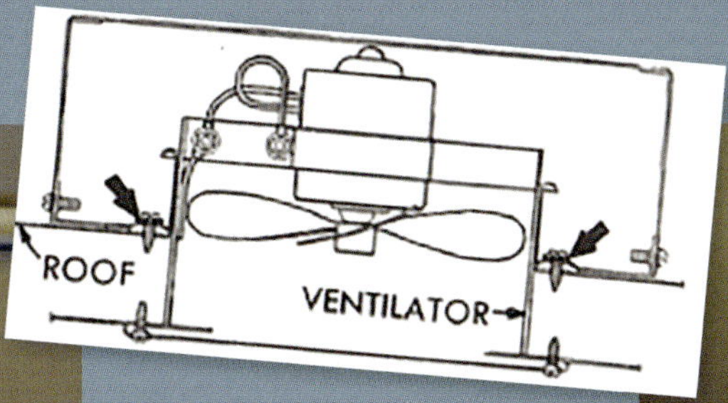

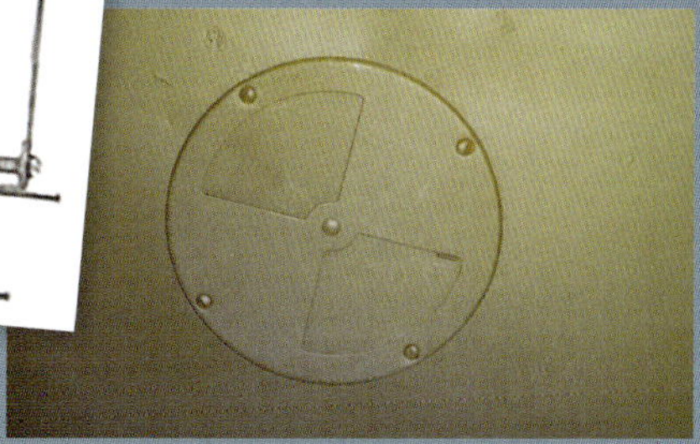

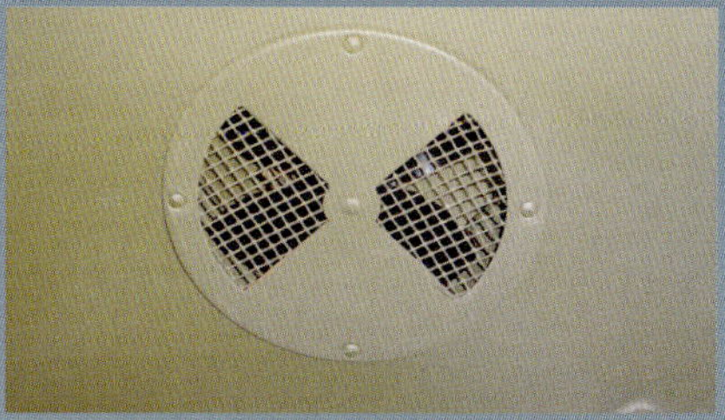

Above: Assembly diagram for the ceiling extractor fan.

Top left: The ceiling light was made of molded glass.

Left: Two-position switches for the extractor fan (left) and the ceiling lights (right).

Top right: Ventilation opening on the ceiling in the closed position.

Center right: Ventilation opening in the open position.

Below: Detailed lists of components for the rear benches compared to the WC27 model.

Bottom left: This view shows the details of the screws for fastening the benches.

Bottom right: Reinforcement fastening panel for the rear benches.

	YEAR AND ENGINEERING SYMBOL	SEAT Assembly Complete—No Irons Longitudinal		BOARD Longitudinal Side Seat		COVER Longitudinal Side Seat		Jute PAD—4" Longitudinal Side Seat		Jute PAD—5" Longitudinal Side Seat		Cotton PAD Bottom Longitudinal Side Seat		
		Right	Left	Right	Left	Right	Left	Right	Left	Right	Left	Right	Left	
		1 Req'd	1 Req'd	1 Req'd	1 Req'd	1 Req'd	1 Req'd	1 Req'd	1 Req'd	1 Req'd	1 Req'd	1 Req'd	1 Req'd	
DODGE WC27 ⇨	1941—T215	⊠9038A	⊠9039A	⊠	⊠	⊠7575	⊠7844	⊠7702	⊠7842	⊠7703	⊠7843	☆	☆	
DODGE WC54 ⇨	1942—T214	9600A	9601A	9602	9603	9805	7575	☆	☆	☆	☆	9996	9659	

Above: Extractor fan; the electricity supply wire is linked to an insulated supply terminal block; it was earthed through a screw on a tab on the engine mounting.

There was an obvious difference between the benches in the Dodge WC54 and its predecessor, the WC27. The WC54's benches had only one layer of filling compared with two for the WC27. There was an obvious difference in thickness between them. It is probable the first WC54 ambulance models coming off the production lines were equipped with benches from the WC27 to get rid of existing stock.

In 1942, the Automotive Council for War Production announced the production of essential materials for making vehicles—like steel, aluminum, rubber and canvas—would be reduced. At the same time, the Army Supply Program's objective was to produce more than three million vehicles of all types from then to July 1944. Manufacturers therefore had to stretch supplies further.

The forecasts were for almost a million vehicles in 1942, more than a million in 1943, and more than a million during the first six months of 1944.

As a result, to avoid shortages, as well as to reduce the padding used, it is possible the rear seat covers were made of faux leather after 1942 as this material had the same qualities as canvas and was used for camping gear and other equipment.

Above: Munich, Germany, 1945. This image was taken from a color film. It shows the thin brown bench. (*Critical Past, License 65685047580*)

Bottom left: France, 1945. This shot was also taken from a color film. The brown bench is visible. (*Critical Past, License 65675070335*)

Below: The bench folded down for use by sitting wounded.

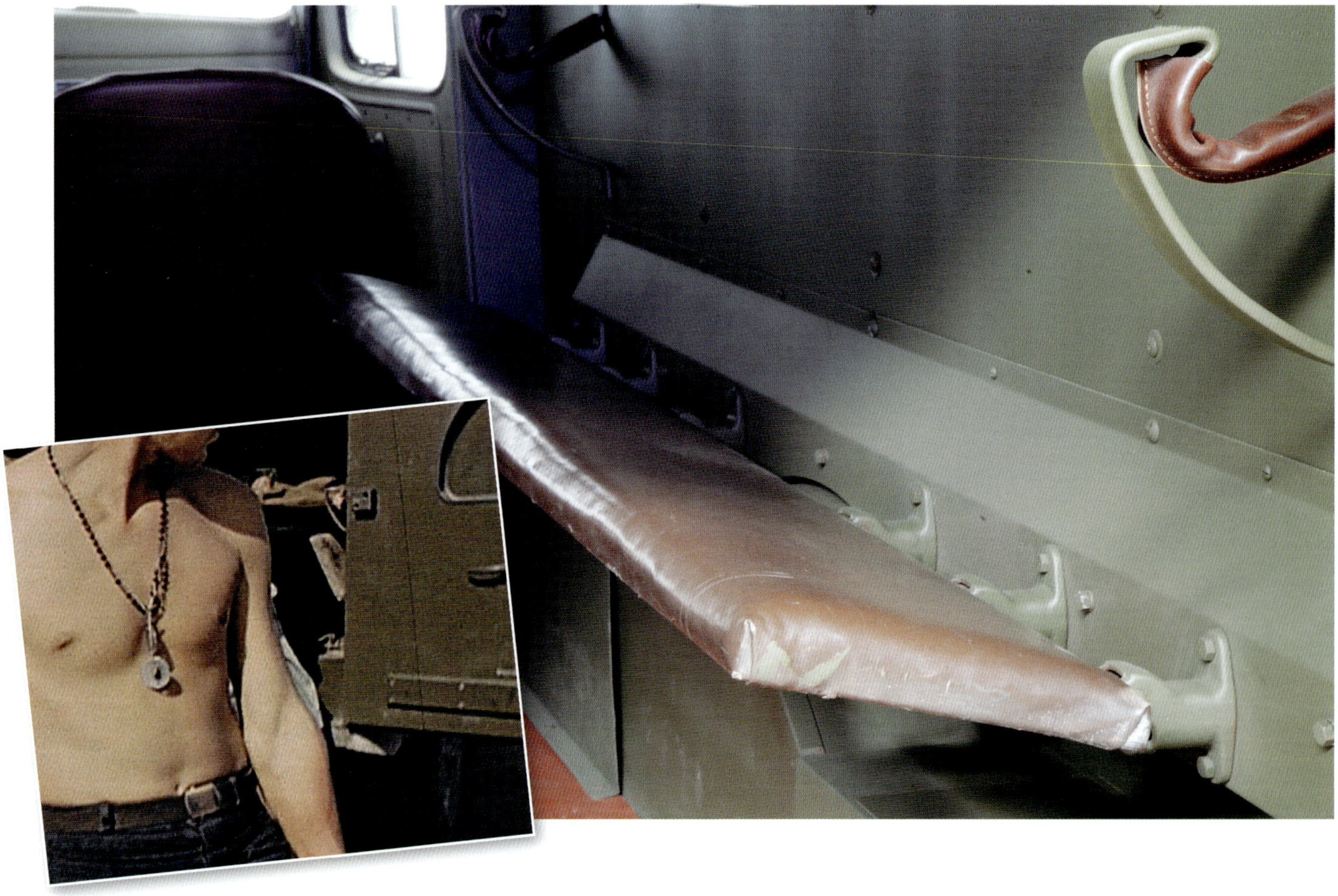

Above: September 1943. The thinness of the bench reveals it surely has an faux leather covering.

Right: Southern France, 1944. This shot is taken from a color film. It shows a brown bench in the background. (*Critical Past, License 65675078080*)

Below right: New Caledonia, 21 December 1944. This view of the bench shows the nails affixing its covering. (*Signal Corps*)

Below: Note how the screw heads are different on every other screw.

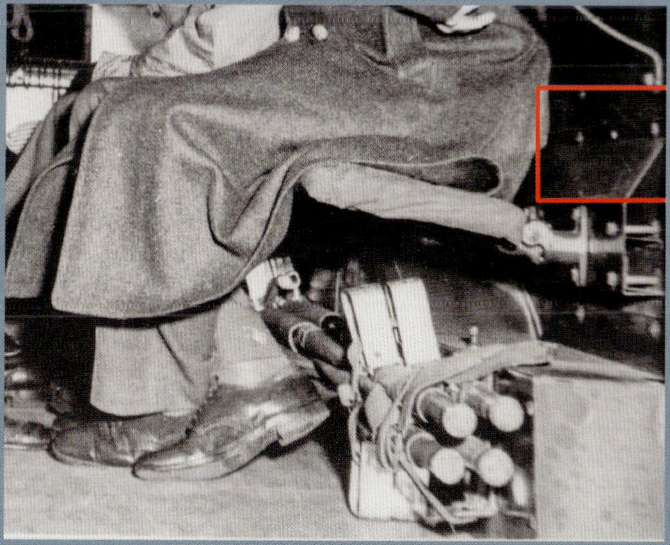

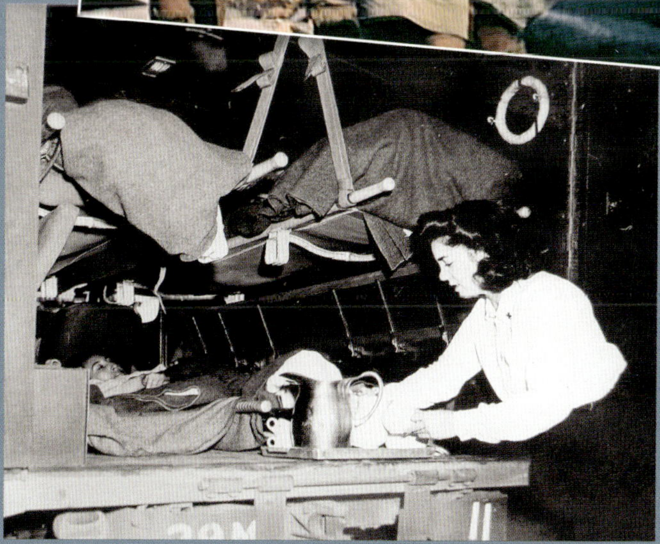

The covering was nailed to the wooden support, not stapled. The stapled covers are the result of restored or reconstructed benches. Canvas benches were also seen on the postwar S7MA51 model.

Bench brackets and springs

The rear benches had two types of brackets supporting them, one with a spring (9194) and the other without (9193). For the long bench, four brackets with springs, and two without, were needed. The shorter bench (on the driver's side) needed four brackets with springs and one without.

Some folding systems were modified by removing the stop to allow the bench to fold back closer to the side. This was a modification carried out by the French Army postwar.

Storage boxes

The ambulance was equipped with three storage boxes. They had four openings covered by removable lids. Each lid was fitted with a simple quarter-turn handle and secured by a small chain. The lids could thus not be easily lost or stolen. The chains consisted of oval links and were attached to the screws of the stretcher strap guard on the inside of the box. The complete assembly of lid and chain was referenced as 7834A. The boxes were attached by four roundhead screws at the rear.

Left: The unpainted bench bracket has been modified by removing the stop.

Bottom: The rear bench retaining arm. The left-hand arm is the model fitted with a spring.

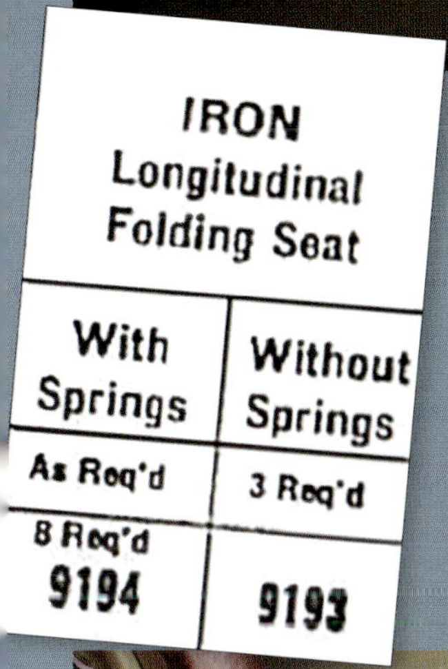

Above: Storage box access panel with its quarter-turn handle.

Left: SNL G657—references of the mechanisms allowing the rear bench to return to its position.

Right: The first type of storage box modified for the second type of stretcher attachment and, finally, the French modification of an oblong opening above the U-shaped holding attachment for slipping the strap through from the inside out.

Below right: The chain preventing the lid from getting lost.

Below left: The cut-out enabled it to hold the bottom of a splint. The boxes were fixed by four roundhead screws on the vertical end. The latter was held on the floor by two hexagonal screws and also welded to the upright of the body.

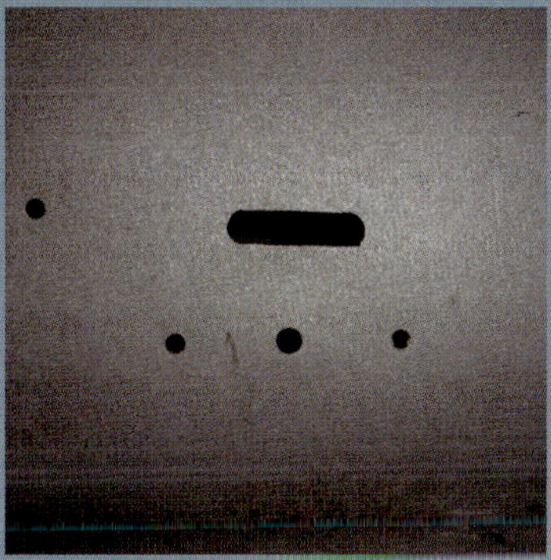

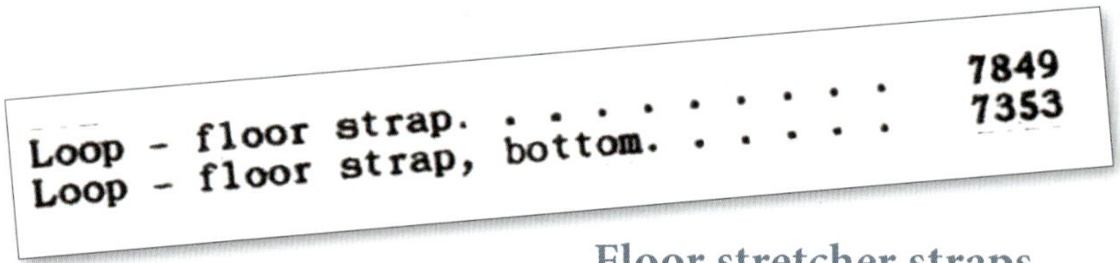
Loop - floor strap. 7849
Loop - floor strap, bottom. 7353

Above: Details of the stretcher strap loops for attaching to the first box models.

Floor stretcher straps

When the stretchers were not in use, they were folded and attached to the boxes by four floor straps.

There were two systems of stretcher floor straps:

- the first consisted of four strap loops (7353) attached by a screw.
- the second consisted of four strap guards (7849)

In both configurations, there were three 7849 guards on the top of the box.

The straps, referenced under number 11334A, were fastened with a stamped buckle. There were two models for the different types of attachment.

The TM9-808 of 15 August 1944 modified the attachment system for the stretcher floor straps. This was a replacement solution for the first attachment model.

Modification of the stretcher strap system

1. In trying to slide two litters (stretchers) on the floor of the ambulance, interference occurs between the litter legs, and the rear litter strap and the bracket assembly. This is particularly true on the older type wooden litters (the legs on the later type litters have been changed to provide additional side clearance). Because of this interference, it is necessary to lift the litter over the rear floor strap bracket before the litter can be slid into place.
2. To prevent interference between rear floor litter strap brackets and litter legs, interchange the rear floor litter strap brackets and the brackets mounted on top of the locker boxes on the sides of the body. To do this, proceed as follows.
   a. Use same center line for this installation. Drill one $^{11}/_{32}$-inch hole in the top of the locker box. This hole should be 7½ inches from the end of the locker, and one inch from the outer edge.

Below: Stretchers in the folded position.

Above: Italy, October 1944. Details of the first model of strap as well as the stamped buckle. (*NARA, American Red Cross*)

Left: This shot shows the 7849 guard well on the spare wheel recess. (*NARA*)

Right: Details of the first type of strap attachment. This is in fact the experimental WC54.

Above left: First type of attachment strap. The strap was sewn with the buckle.

Above right: Second type of strap for attaching the stretchers to the floor. The buckle has been painted white during a renovation.

Below: Detail of the floor stretcher straps on the spare wheel recess.

Left: Second type of strap for holding the stretcher to the floor.

Right: First type of strap for holding the stretcher when not in use.

Below: Details of the folded straps of the second model.

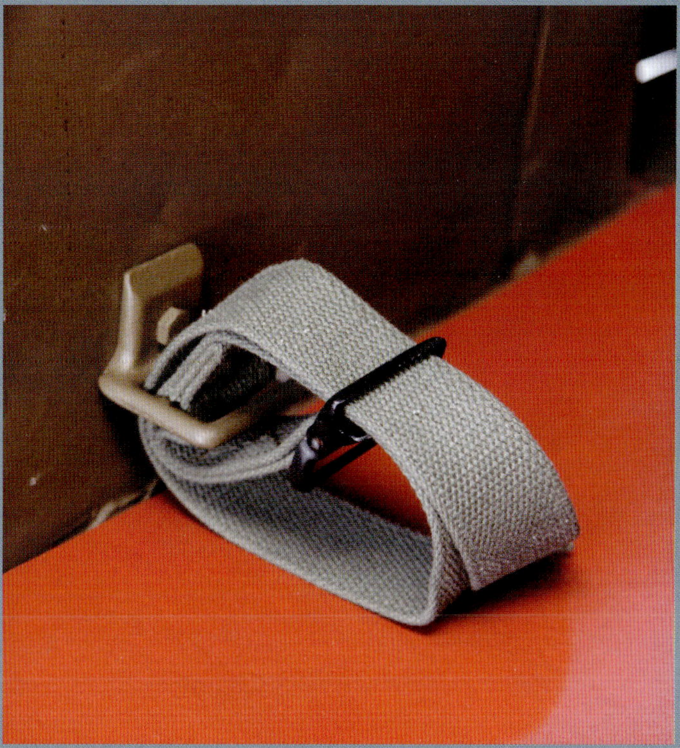

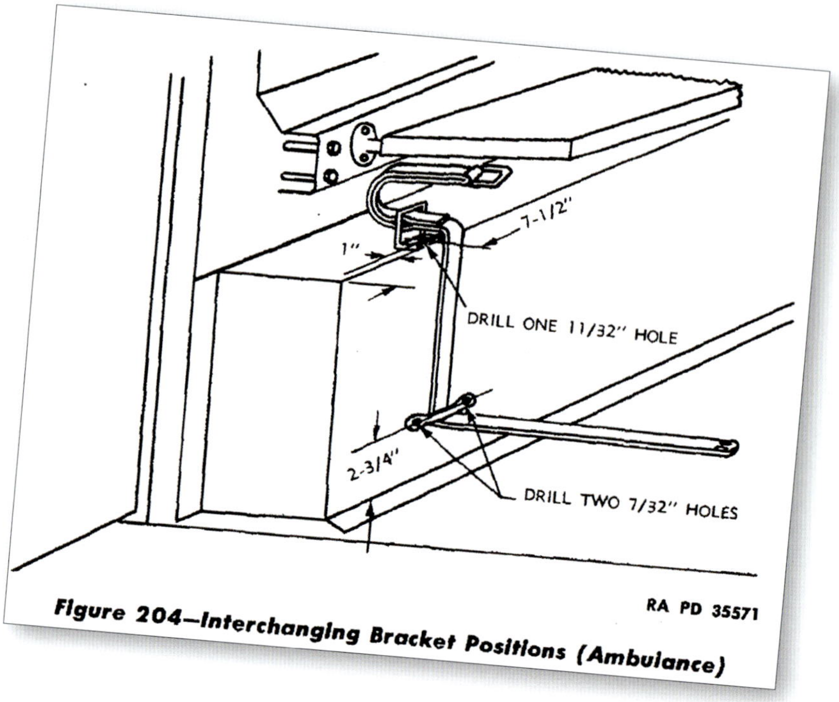

Figure 204—Interchanging Bracket Positions (Ambulance)

b. Drill two 7/32-inch holes in the side of the locker box for the bracket that was on the top of the locker box. These holes should be 2¾ inches from the floor of the vehicle.

c. Install the strap and brackets in the same manner as shown … using the same attaching bolts.

d. This correction should be performed on both sides of the body in the rear.

Rear crossbar

The rear crossbar enabled the floor mat of the body to be held in place by pinching. It received the attachments for the axle pivots of the rear footstep foldable brackets.

Canvas strips on the interior wheel arches

The inside panels near the wheel arches were trimmed. The canvas strip was placed between the wheel and the inside panel and was 53½ inches long on the right and 47½ inches on the left.

The bracket recess for the spare wheel had no weltcord.

Canvas strip for external wheel arches

The outside rear wheel arches were joined to the bodywork by a canvas weltcord (9676). This prevented water and dust infiltrating the walls. It was held in place by sheet metal screws from the inside of the wheel arches. This weltcord was 64½ inches long on the right and 52½ inches on the left.

Exterior Bodywork

Hood

The engine hood was specific to the ambulance models and Carryalls. It had no windshield fixing points and its slope was more pronounced.

Dodge grille plate

The plate with the Dodge name (CC991214) was affixed to the front of the grille up to chassis 81542677 and also on the series 81550001–

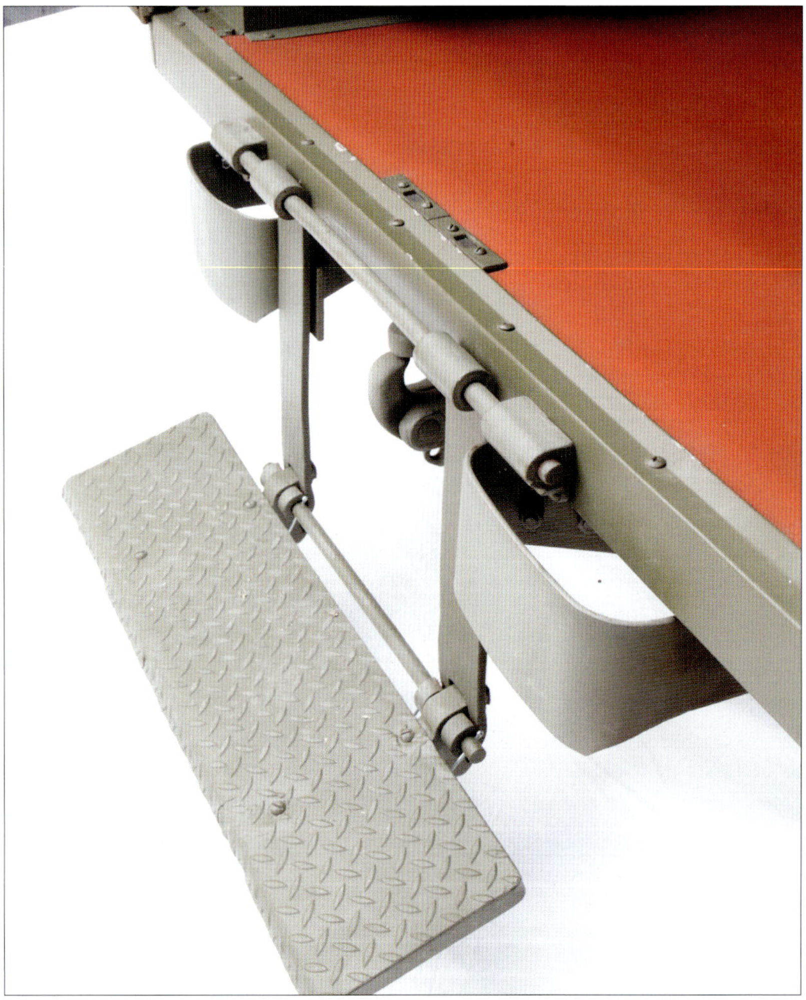

Left: Footstep folded down for use.

Above: Under the benches on each side, the weltcord can be seen between the wheel arch and the side panel. This runs down to the bottom of the box

WELTCORD Wheelhouse to Side Panel			
Outside		Inside	
Right	Left	Right	Left
1 Req'd	1 Req'd	1 Req'd	1 Req'd
9676-64½	9676-52½	9676-53½	9676-47½

Left: Weltcord references and lengths for the inside and outside wheel arches.

Right: Canvas weltcord positioned between the wheel arch and the panel.

81553006. After these rolled off the assembly line, subsequent vehicles did not have a plate.

External side panels

The side panels were made of a single piece with a rib stamped along the middle.

It is possible to come across screwed panels. This was common practice with the ERGM restorations by the French Army. Be careful though. When restoring, the presence of back plates is often a sign the original sheet metal has deteriorated. It has often been attacked by rust; these plates must be removed.

Removing water from the air trap door

As with all the Dodges in the WC series, the WC54 was equipped with an air intake, located in front of the windshield and protected by a trapdoor. It fitted the metal cabin and, to get rid of the water which managed to infiltrate, a drainpipe (CC950630) went through the firewall.

Gutters

In order to avoid water streaming down the side of the vehicle, the WC54 was fitted with gutters all around the roof. The gutters above the front doors were made of aluminum alloy and screwed to the bodywork.

Windshield

The windshield consisted of two removable parts joined together by countersunk headed screws. The lower part (CC844630) was often damaged by corrosion.

The two parts of the windshield were joined by two metal clips (CC592882).

Windshield wipers

The windshield wiper arm (CC925407) was adapted for the closed-in cabin. They were different from the open cabs of the Dodge WC series as they were not fitted to the windshield. The arm had a hinge enabling the windshield to be opened, avoiding putting any pressure on the vacuum motor axis, while still keeping the blades flat on the screen. The blades (CC883056) were 8½ inches long.

The hole giving access to the control was protected by a black rubber grommet (CC117957). The windshield wipers functioned by vacuum. The air intake was on the intake manifold. The rubber vacuum pipe, coming from the manifold,

Below: Left-hand side view of the body.

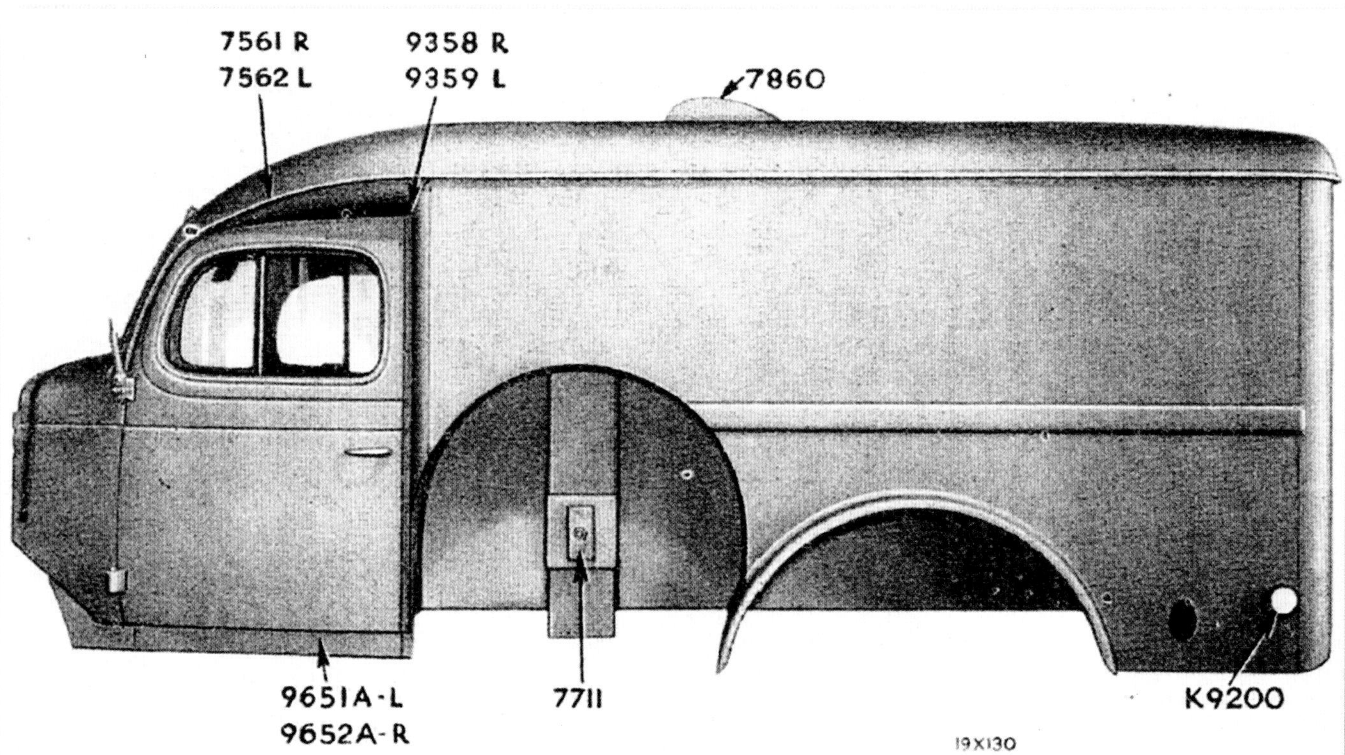

Above: Hoods, except for the WC53 and WC54, were flat and had specific attachment points.

Below: References and dimensions of the water evacuation pipe.

Right: The water evacuation pipe of the ventilation trap door passed through an oblong hole. It was held against the wall by a metal tab.

Bottom: The spare wheel recess has been lined with sheet metal inside and outside to cover bodywork defects.

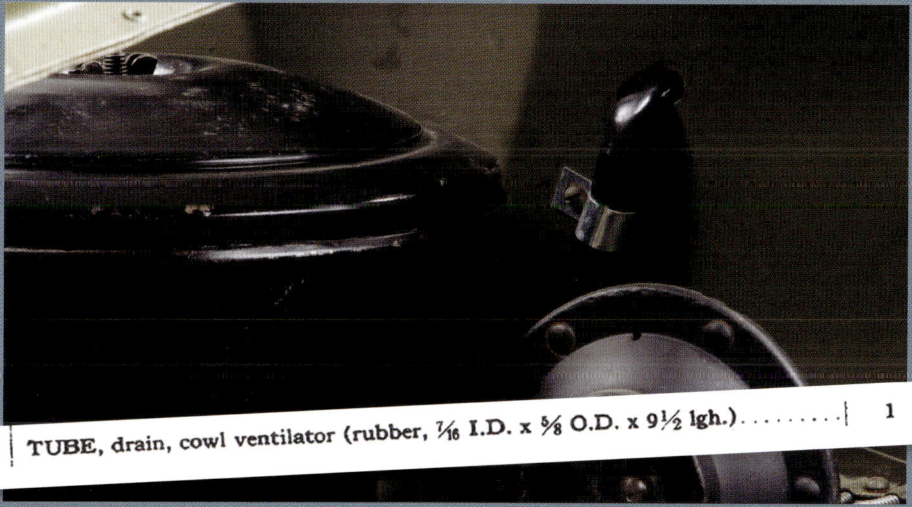

(CC-950630)	(CC-950630)	TUBE, drain, cowl ventilator (rubber, 7/16 I.D. x 5/8 O.D. x 9½ lgh.)........	1

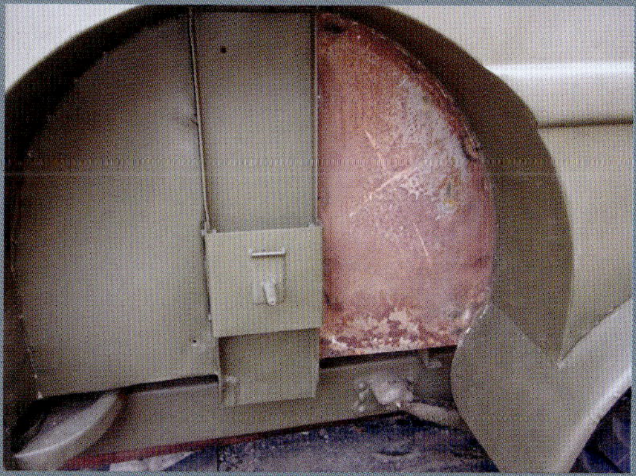

Right: The elements making up the windshield and its opening system.

WINDSHIELD AND PARTS—SUB-GROUP 1801

USM-BODY-1

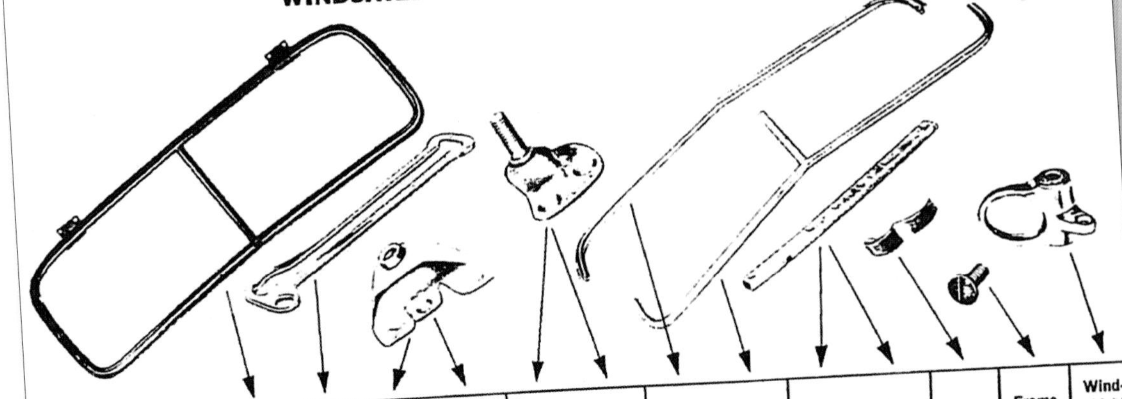

YEAR AND ENGINEERING SYMBOL	WIND-SHIELD Ass'y	Wind-shield Adjust-ing ARM	Adjusting Arm Frame BRACKET Assembly		Adjusting Arm (To Pillar) BRACKET Ass'y		Windshield FRAME Ass'y		Frame Joint TAPPING PLATE		Frame CLIP (Frame Joint)	Frame SCREW (Joint Tapping Plate)	Wind-shield Pull-To HAN-DLE
			Right	Left	Right	Left	Upper	Lower	Right	Left			
		A	SEE NOTE 1	SEE NOTE 1	B	B							
	1 Req'd	2 Req'd	1 Req'd	1 Req'd	1 Req'd	1 Req'd	1 Req'd	1 Req'd	1 Req'd	1 Req'd	2 Req'd	8 Req'd	1 Req'd
1942—T214	966456	922889	889090	889091	☆	☆	844630	844631	902925	902926	592882	844528	45239

Below left:

1. Windshield wiper body check
2. Assembling paddle to motor shaft
3. Placing paddle in the forming tray
4. Inserting paddle in wiper body

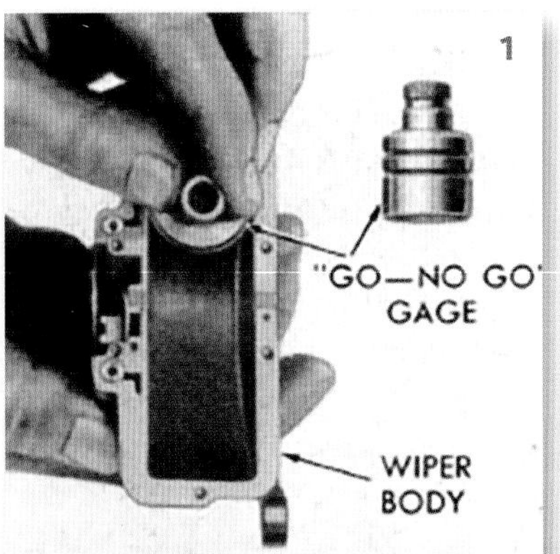

CHECKING WIPER BODY WITH "GO—NO GO" GAGE

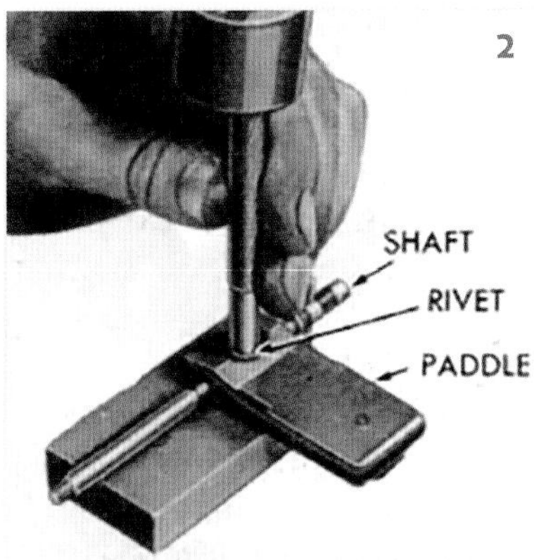

ASSEMBLY OF PADDLE TO SHAFT

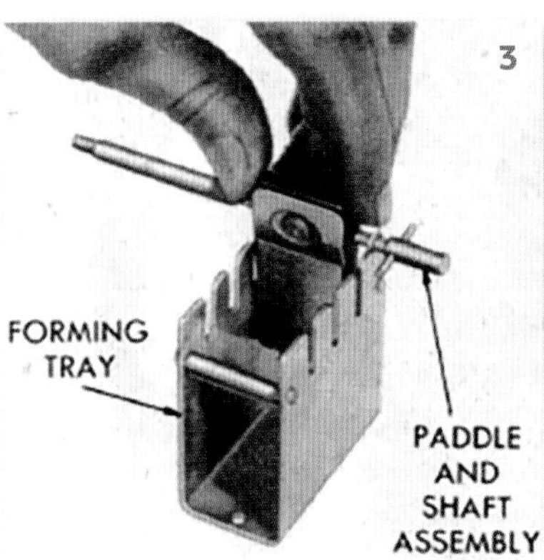

PLACING PADDLE IN FORMING TRAY

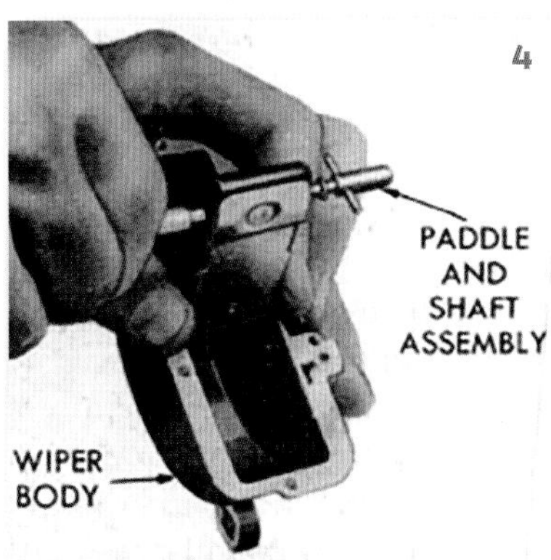

INSERTING PADDLE IN WIPER BODY

went through the top and was protected by a rubber grommet (CC120879). It went up through the front forward bodywork upright and was connected to a brass distributor to power the two motors. The motors were made by Trico. The connection of the vacuum pipe was on the right side of the motor.

Below: Positions of the windshield wiper motors.

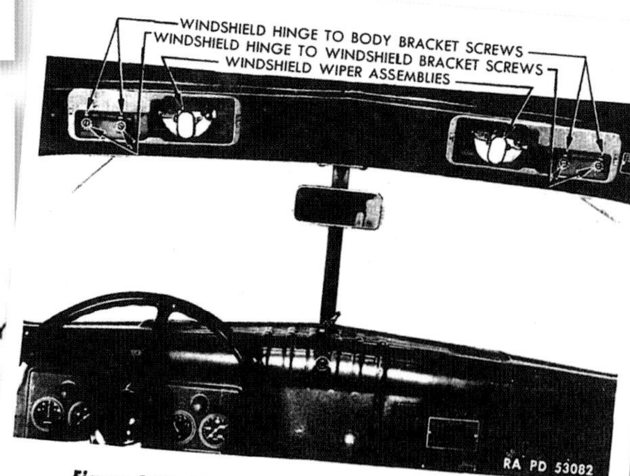

Figure 203—Windshield Hinge and Wiper Location (Closed Bodies)

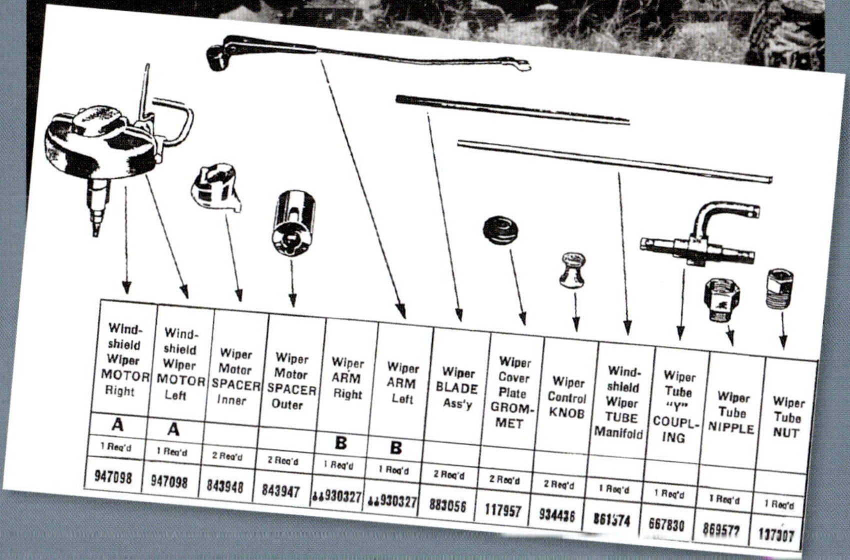

Wind-shield Wiper MOTOR Right	Wind-shield Wiper MOTOR Left	Wiper Motor SPACER Inner	Wiper Motor SPACER Outer	Wiper ARM Right	Wiper ARM Left	Wiper BLADE Ass'y	Wiper Cover Plate GROM-MET	Wiper Control KNOB	Wind-shield Wiper TUBE Manifold	Wiper Tube "Y" COUPL-ING	Wiper Tube NIPPLE	Wiper Tube NUT
A	A			B	B							
1 Req'd	1 Req'd	2 Req'd	2 Req'd	1 Req'd	1 Req'd	2 Req'd	2 Req'd	2 Req'd	1 Req'd	1 Req'd	1 Req'd	1 Req'd
947098	947098	843948	843947	930327	930327	883056	117957	934436	861574	667830	869577	137307

Above: This profile shot enables us to see the hinge on the windshield wiper arm.

Top right: Burma, November 1944. The windshield is wide open showing the need for specific windshield wiper arms. (*NARA*)

Right: All the elements making up the windshield wiper system. The SNL gives the reference here as CC930327 which corresponds to the repair kit for the arm and the adaptors for various motors. The arm's reference is CC925407.

Below and right: Pipe grommets for protecting the windscreen wiper motors.

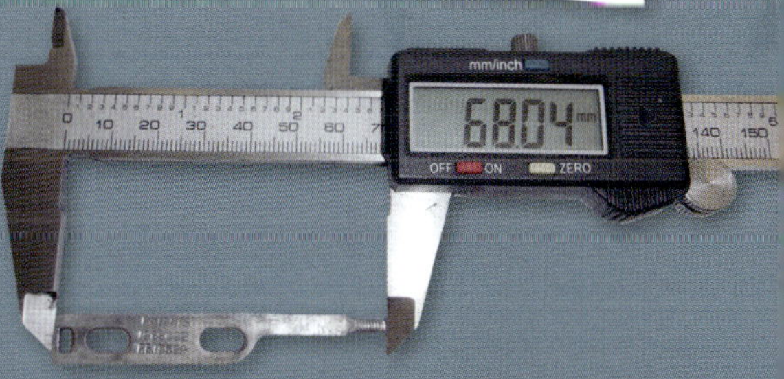

Above: This control is suitable and enables it to be used with the rubber grommet.

Below: The length of this control lever is not adapted to being fitted on the WC54 when the cache has a rubber grommet.

A specific kit for renovating windshield motors exists with the reference TRI 5P1065X.

Very often the motor spindle does not give the wiper blade enough adherence. Here is a trick to renovate the attachment part. See the series of four photographs on opposite page.

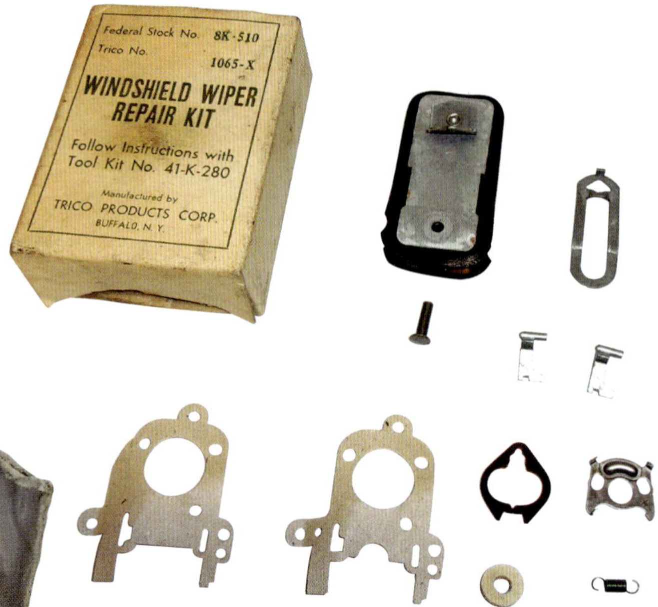

Above: Parts for the repair kit for the windshield wiper motors specific to the WC53 and WC54.

Below: Tool kit for renovating the wiper motors. It can be used on several models of motors.

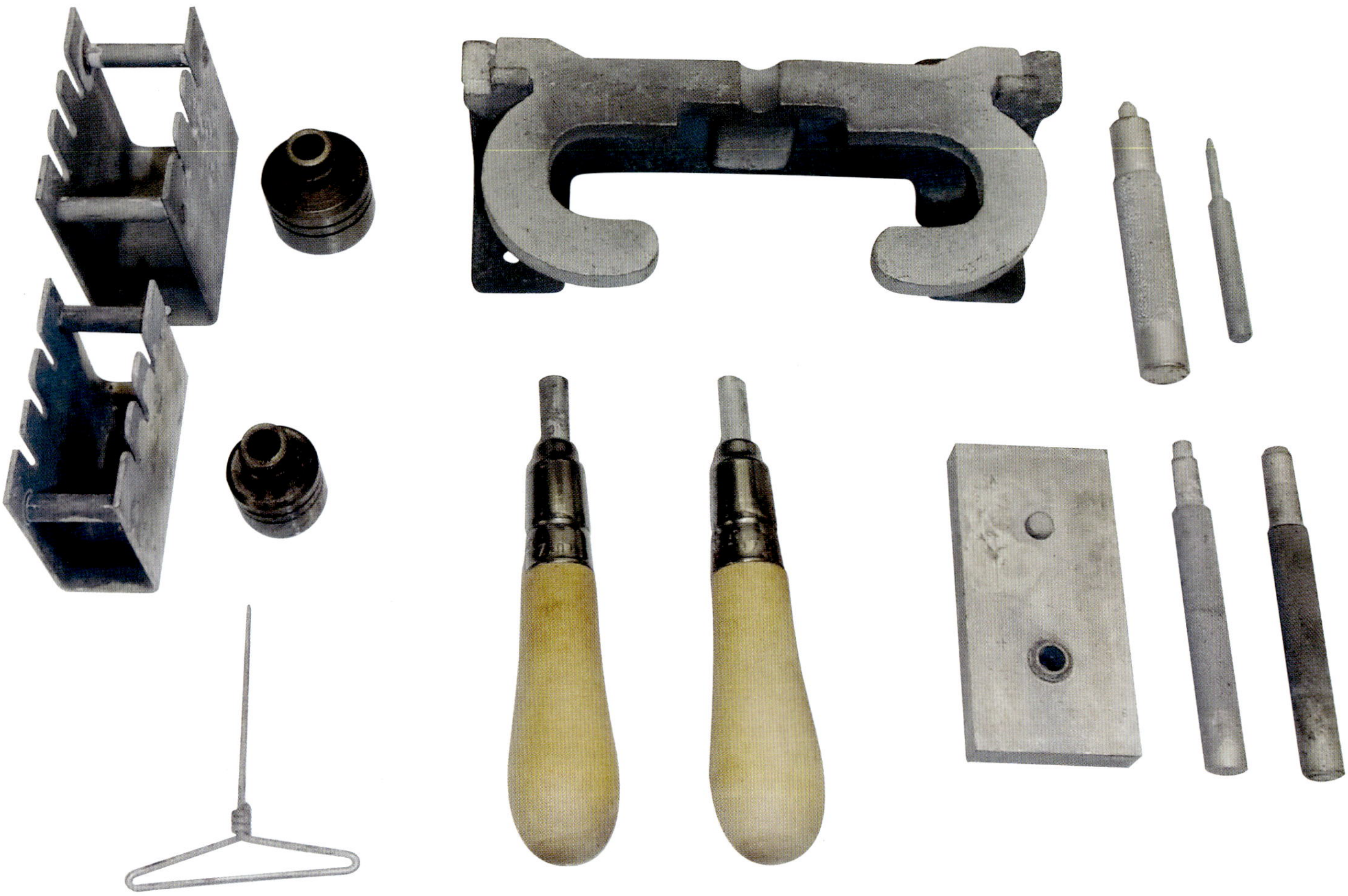

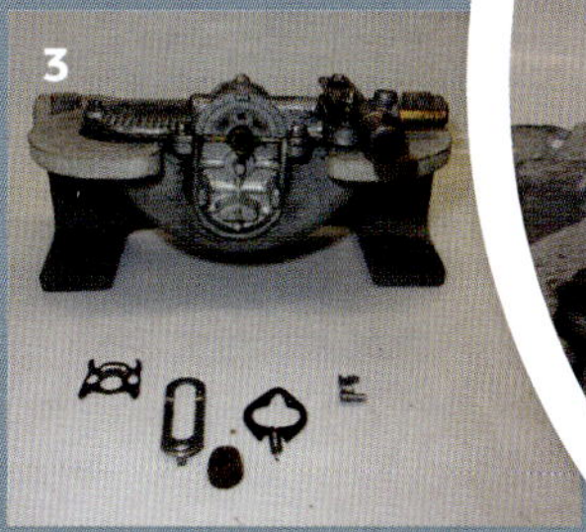

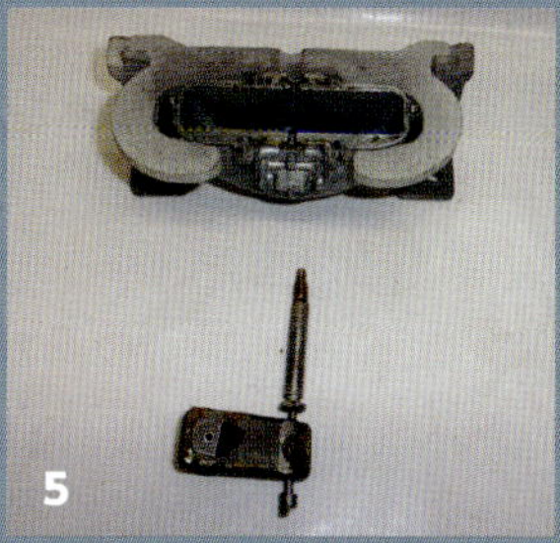

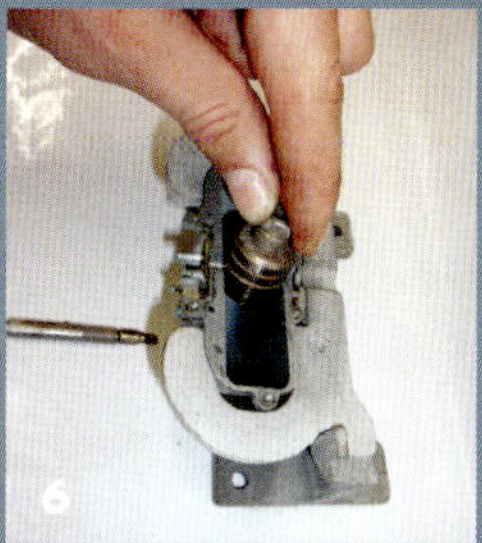

Stripping down

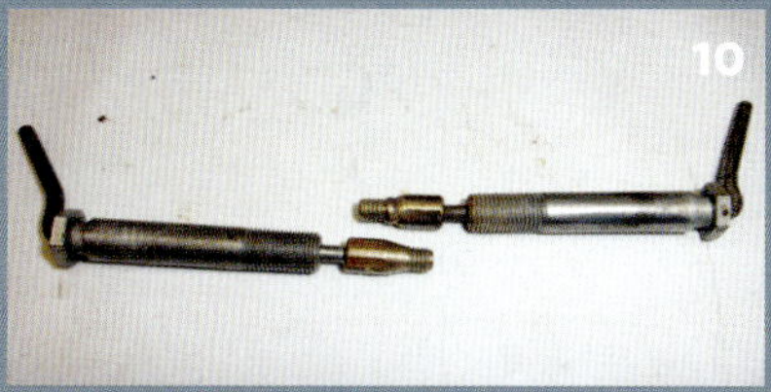

1. The motor is in place on the special support.
2. Remove the protective flange from the mechanism.
3. Remove the elements of the mechanism. All the components are to be found in the renovation kit
4. Remove the six screws holding the motor cover.
5. Remove the arm and its flap.
6. Use the wear gauge; it has three dimensions.
7. Disassembled arm and shutter.
8. Clip enabling the sweeping movement of the wiper. There were two types (89° and 110°) allowing different angles. The ambulance uses 89°.
9. Dismantled flap and new flap from the kit.
10. The support bracket is worn; this will be replaced.

Reassembly

1. Reassembling the flap using the crimped rivet.
2. Setting up the flap before putting it in place.
3. The arm and flap in place. During the following steps, regularly check the flap moves correctly.
4. These elements are calibrated for working at 89° or 107°.

4–9. Reassembling the movement mechanism parts.

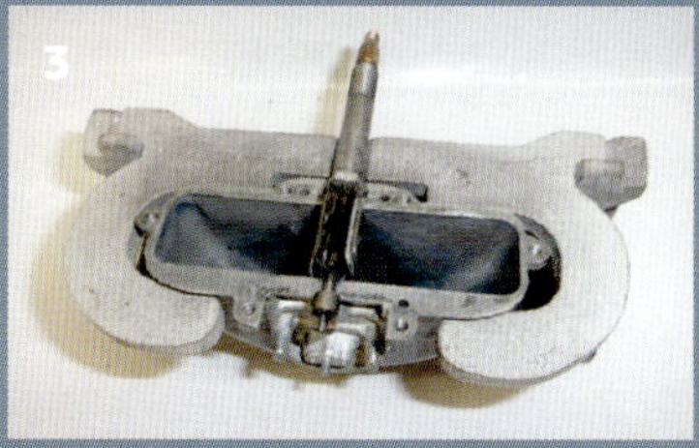

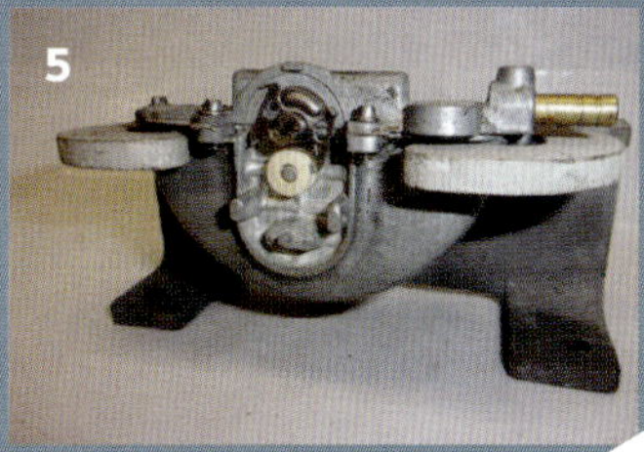

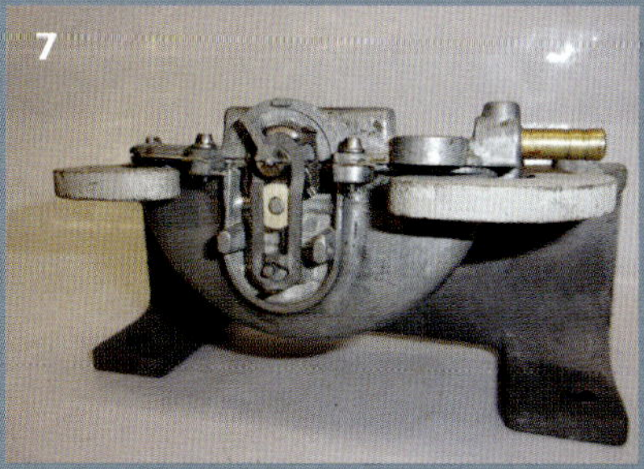

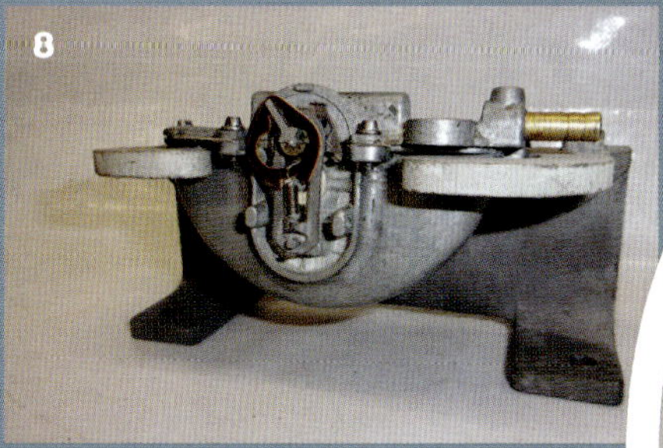

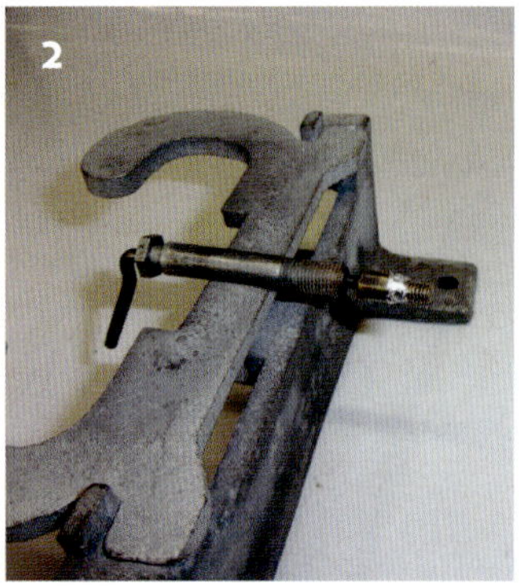

Left:
1. Damaged shaft.
2. After cleaning and degreasing the shaft, heat the part to be filled with a soldering iron, get rid of excess tin.

3–4. File down the excess, respecting the angle; the wiper arms will regain their proper adherence.

Spare wheel bracket

The spare wheel bracket is an integral part of the bodywork.

The wheel is held by a flat metal bracket and held in place by a strong U-shaped profile (7711), fastened with a wheel nut.

Filler and fuel tank

The fuel tank is identical to that on the Carryall or Command WC series of vehicles.

There were two types of fuel tanks:

- The first (CC925044) was stamped, with two elements welded together. It had a small filler neck.
- The second (CC928084) was rectangular and had a big filler cap. It was fitted on chassis 81625758 onwards, 81625256 and the 81625472–81625734 range.

The two types of filler pipe were installed in different body panel styles on the left rear corner. For the smaller pipe, a simple hole to fit the neck was all that was required. A piece of rectangular leather filled the space between the neck and the bodywork.

Below: Firenzuola, Italy, 25 February 1945. Smooth side panel with the small fuel filler hole.

Above: Le Reno, Praduro, Italy, 21 April 1945. The large filler cap is evident here, as is the useful recess in the panel.

Far right: Spare wheel position.

Right: Instructions for setting up the spare wheel in its specified place.

Below center: The nook for the second model of filler neck.

Below right: Second model of fuel tank.

Below: Mounting for the large filler cap. This unit was mounted on the bodywork.

WHEELS AND TIRES

FIRST POSITION

SECOND POSITION

THIRD POSITION

FINAL POSITION

RA PD 58369

Figure 183—Installing Spare Wheel on Carrier

For the other model, the bodywork was modified by adding a recess for the big filler cap as well as a ventilation hole to make filling the tank from a jerry can easier. The neck had a mounting on this model.

Front doors

The front doors were particular to the ambulance. They consisted of a vertical sliding window with a non-sliding deflector at the front.

The doors with a one-piece window were characteristic of the Carryall (WC53). The ambulances were never fitted with a single-piece window. Again, these were postwar French Army or civilian modifications. A door with a one-piece window could not be equipped with a deflector pane.

The ambulance doors had, respectively, the parts numbers CC909323 and CC909322.

The pane went up and down between two flexible runs, guided by a rigid channel in the bottom at the front end of the door, and attached by screws to the armature of the door, with another at the rear. The pane was surrounded by a metal frame to make moving and guiding easier. In order to avoid contact between the pane and the metal parts, the latter was covered with a runner preventing premature wear when the pane moved up and down.

The doors had slots for rubber pads, dampening the sideways movements of the pane. According to the nomenclature of the WC54, however, the ambulances were not fitted with them. These were certainly door components manufactured for the WC27 and reused on the WC54.

Each front door had a retention arm for opening and dampening movement in normal use. These were equipped with a cylindrical pad (CC797109) and a rectangular piece of rubber (CC785987) riveted to the bodywork upright through which the arm passed. The retention arm was fixed to the door with a caulked rivet (CC706148).

In order to dampen impact of the closing door, two pads (CC399526) were fixed to the upright of the bodywork.

Right: Details of the front window mechanisms.

Below: The slots for the side pads. These were absent on the WC54 model.

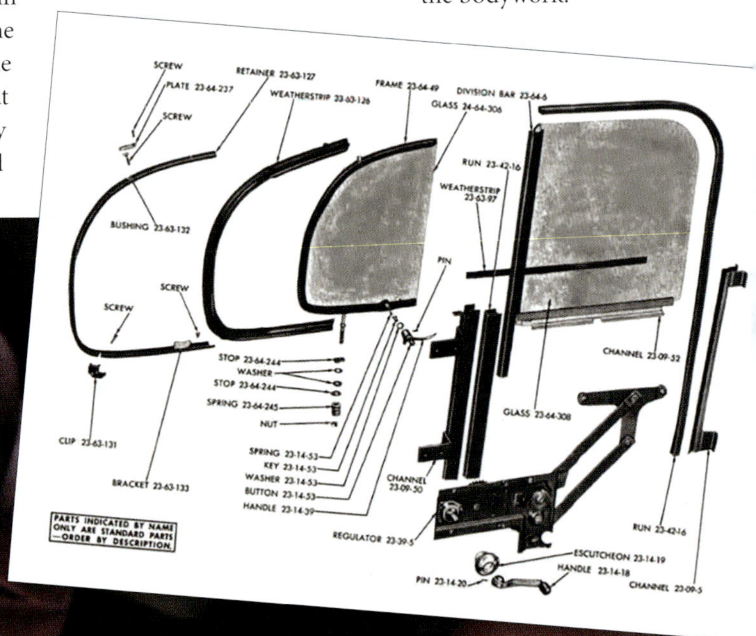

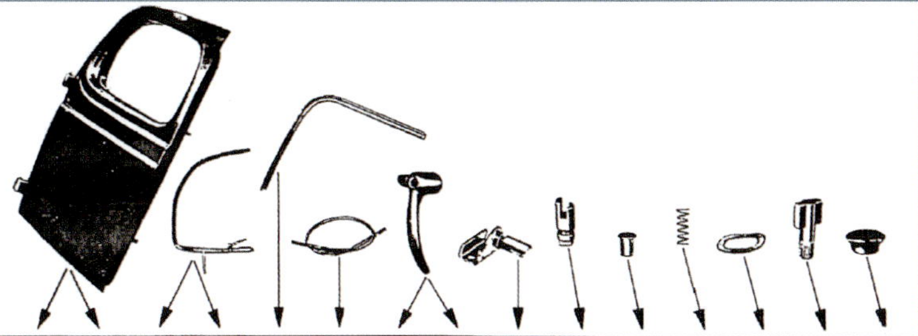

Front Door SHELL Assembly		Vent. Wing Glass FRAME		Window Glass FRAME	Window Glass Frame FILLER	Vent. Window HANDLE		Vent. Window Handle SHAFT and BRACKET Ass'y (Handle)	Vent. Window Handle SHAFT Only	Vent. Window RIVET (Bracket to Frame)	Vent. Window Handle SPRING	Vent. Window Handle WASHER	Vent. Window Handle KEY	Vent. Window Handle BUTTON
Right	Left	Right	Left			Right	Left							
				A		B	B							
1 Req'd	1 Req'd	1 Req'd	1 Req'd	2 Req'd	2 Req'd	1 Req'd	1 Req'd	2 Req'd	2 Req'd	4 Req'd	2 Req'd	2 Req'd	2 Req'd	2 Req'd
909322	909323	909292	909293	909256	909257	939181	939182	850664	767693	492365	763705	764211	792416	939178

AMBULANCE

CARRYALL

Part No.	PART NAME	Model Codes 4290	4219	4229	4239	4249	4266	List Price
	FRONT DOOR SHELL ASSEMBLY							
909322	Right	...	...	...	1	...	...	27.50
909359	Right	...	...	...	...	1	...	27.50
909323	Left.	...	...	...	1	...	...	27.50
909360	Left.	...	...	...	...	1	...	27.50

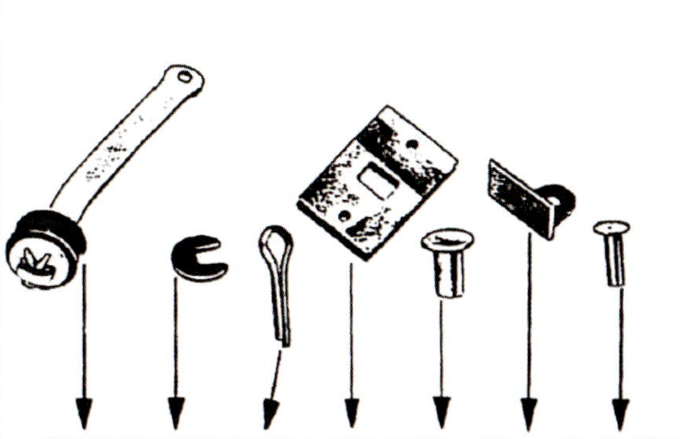

Front Door Check ARM Ass'y	Check Arm WASHER	Check Arm PIN	Check Arm Bumper STOP	Check Arm RIVET (Stop)	Check Arm BRACKET	Check Arm Bracket RIVET
2 Req'd	2 Req'd	2 Req'd	2 Req'd	4 Req'd	4 Req'd	2 Req'd
797109	326239	103394	785987	728150	785981	706148

Top: Front door assemblies including elements of the deflector window.

Above: Reference table for ambulance and Carryall doors.

Above right: Details of elements making up the front door retainers.

Right: Rubber parts for dampening the front doors.

Bottom right: Rubber parts for the front door retainer arm, the cylindrical part has disappeared with time.

Below: The knob on the window winder was made of molded plastic.

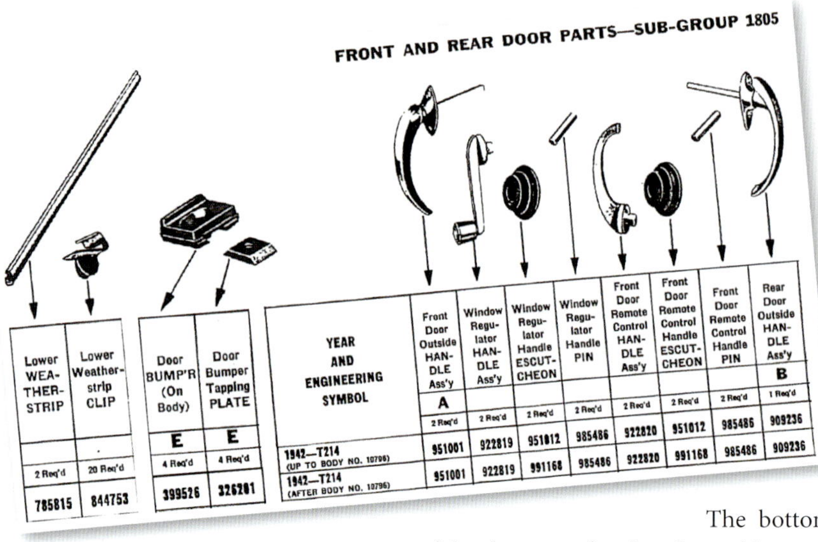

FRONT AND REAR DOOR PARTS—SUB-GROUP 1805

Lower WEA-THER-STRIP	Lower Weather-strip CLIP
	·
2 Req'd	20 Req'd
785815	844753

Door BUMP'R (On Body)	Door Bumper Tapping PLATE
E	E
4 Req'd	4 Req'd
399526	326281

YEAR AND ENGINEERING SYMBOL	Front Door Outside HAN-DLE Ass'y	Window Regu-lator HAN-DLE Ass'y	Window Regu-lator Handle ESCUT-CHEON	Window Regu-lator Handle PIN	Front Door Remote Control HAN-DLE Ass'y	Front Door Remote Control Handle ESCUT-CHEON	Front Door Remote Control Handle PIN	Rear Door Outside HAN-DLE Ass'y
	A							B
	2 Req'd	2 Req'd	2 Req'd	2 Req'd	2 Req'd	2 Req'd	2 Req'd	1 Req'd
1942—T214 (UP TO BODY NO. 10796)	951001	922819	951012	985486	922820	951012	985486	909236
1942—T214 (AFTER BODY NO. 10796)	951001	922819	991168	985486	922820	991168	985486	909236

The bottom of the door was fitted with a rubber seal (CC844575) held in place by a series of 10 clips (CC844753).

The interior door handles were fitted vertically.

Above,from left: Weather strip located under the front doors with attachment clips; doorstop attached to the body upright; details of the handles for the front and rear doors.

Rear-view mirror

The ambulance was fitted with a single external rear-view mirror (CC919230). It was attached by an arm to the upper door hinge on the driver's side. The arm therefore moved with the door and was jointed for adjustment, moving upwards or downwards, and sideways.

The arm was made by King Bee.

Front and rear door lock cylinders

The ambulance was an emergency vehicle that needed to be secured. It was therefore fitted with locks. The passenger-side door and the rear door were fitted with them. The driver's door did not have one but could be locked from the inside by pushing the door handle to the rear.

The keys were the same for all doors.

Rear doors

The rear doors consisted of two hinged sections.

Below: The handles for opening the doors returned to this vertical position, preventing them from catching equipment or clothing when people got in or out of the vehicle.

Bottom center: Details of the front door handle.

Below: Front door retention arm This was held in place by a flat, caulked rivet.

Below right: Rubber stops for dampening the door as it closed.

Bottom: View of the bottom front door seal held in place by a series of 10 clips and the door sill.

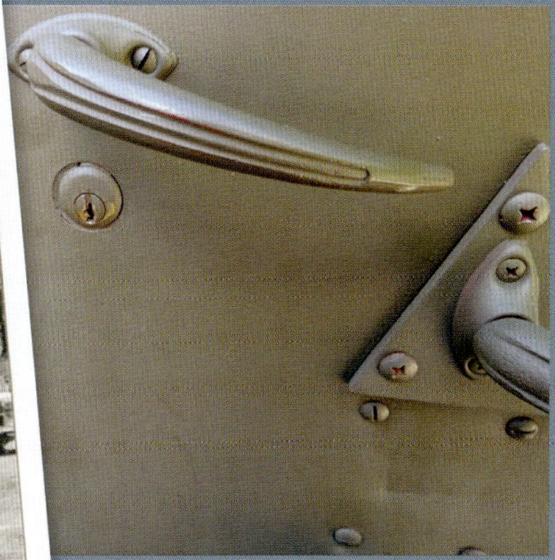

Above: Germany, 1945. A makeshift passenger-side rear-view mirror arm made with a piece of flat steel and most certainly held in place by the door hinge. There is also a tube on the front fender to hold a flag. (*National Library of Scotland—The Portal to Texas History*)

Top center: Lock barrel for the rear door.

Top right: Detailed view of the rear-view mirror attachment point.

Above right: King Bee arm and rear-view mirror.

Right: Oran region, Algeria, October 1943. A volunteer driver from the 531st Medical Company. On the dashboard is the company's mascot. The rear-view mirror is attached to the door hinge and moves with the door. Its mount also includes a hinge, enabling it to be adjusted horizontally and vertically. (*Unknown Photographer, ECPAD /Défense*)

Below: Detailed view of the markings on the King Bee rear-view mirror arm.

Left: England, 21 May 1944. The open door of this 381st Bomb Group ambulance enables us to see its seals. (*NARA*)

Below: References for the rear door seals.

Bottom: Rath, Germany, 13 April 1945. This shot shows the seals on the rear doors clearly. (*NARA*)

Bottom right: References for the seals from the Wayne Works catalogue.

Rubber - rear door seal R.H. door . .	7819	1
Rubber - rear door seal L.H.	7820	1

They were held shut by upper and lower latches and could be locked with a key.

The doors were fitted to the floor by inserting the rods into two plates screwed into the floor. To make sure they were waterproof, a rubber seal (11043) was placed between the plates and the floor.

Rear door seals

The rear doors were fitted with a triangular seal. It went right around the sill of right-hand door. The left-hand door only had this seal on three sides, the central seal being on the other door.

There were two references for each seal because one came from the Wayne Works catalogue and the other from the SNL G502.

The Wayne Works catalogue references were 7819 (right-hand seal) and 7820 (left-hand seal).

Rear door window seals

The seals for the rear windows were made up of two elements: one for keeping the pane in place (11191) and the other filled in the space between the two door panels (11185).

Rear Door SEAL	
Right	Left
1 Req'd	1 Req'd
11144	11145

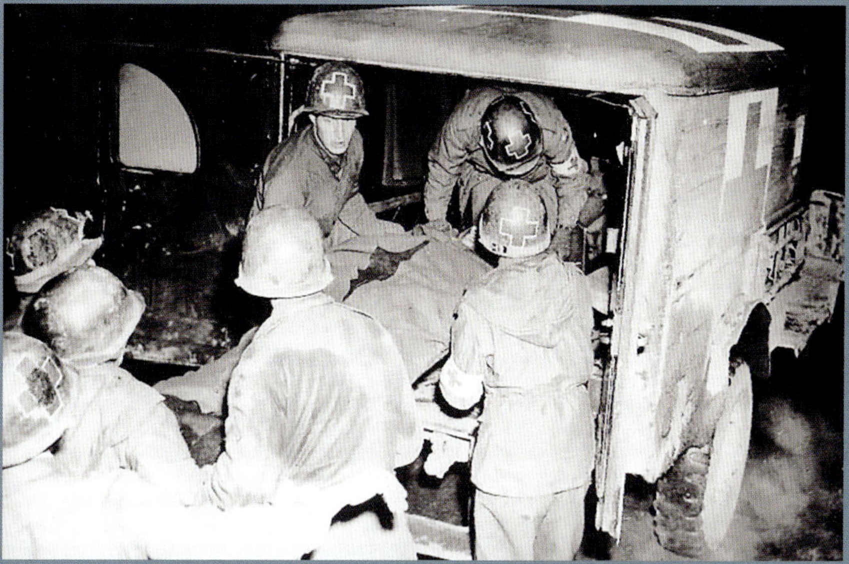

Top: Overall view of the rear doors. Phillips-head screws were already in use at the time.

Above: Rubber seals blocking the holes in the floor were held in place by the plate fastenings.

Above right: The triangular seal can be seen on the top of the door.

Right: Rear door lined with sheet metal. Removing it reveals the damage.

Below: Inside rear view, left.

Below right: Inside rear view, right.

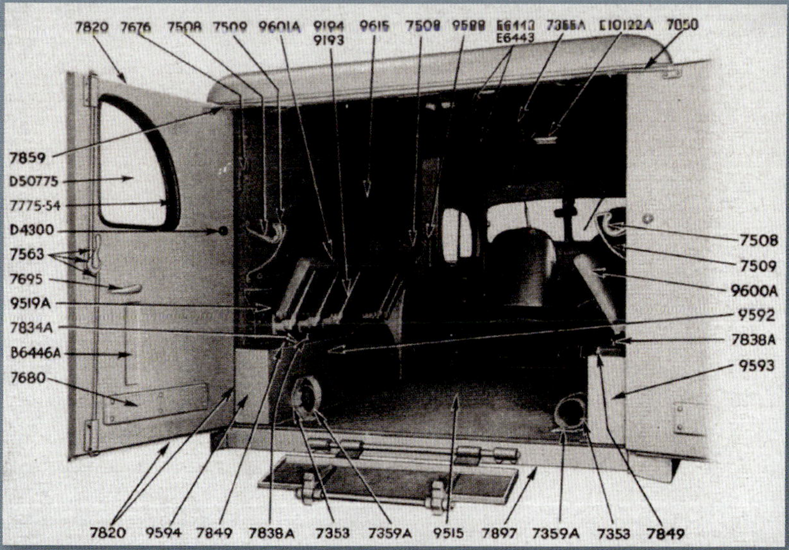

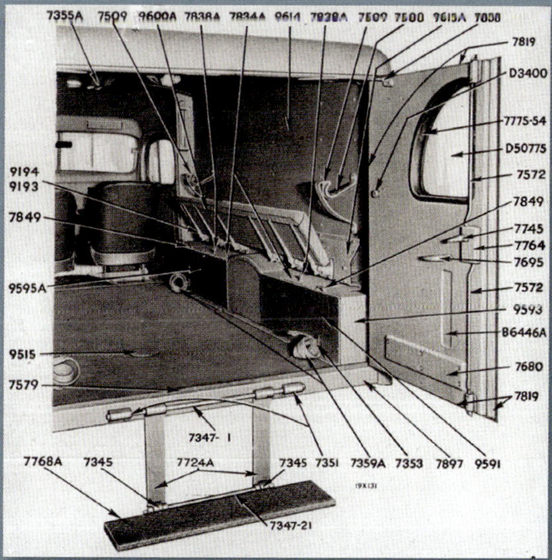

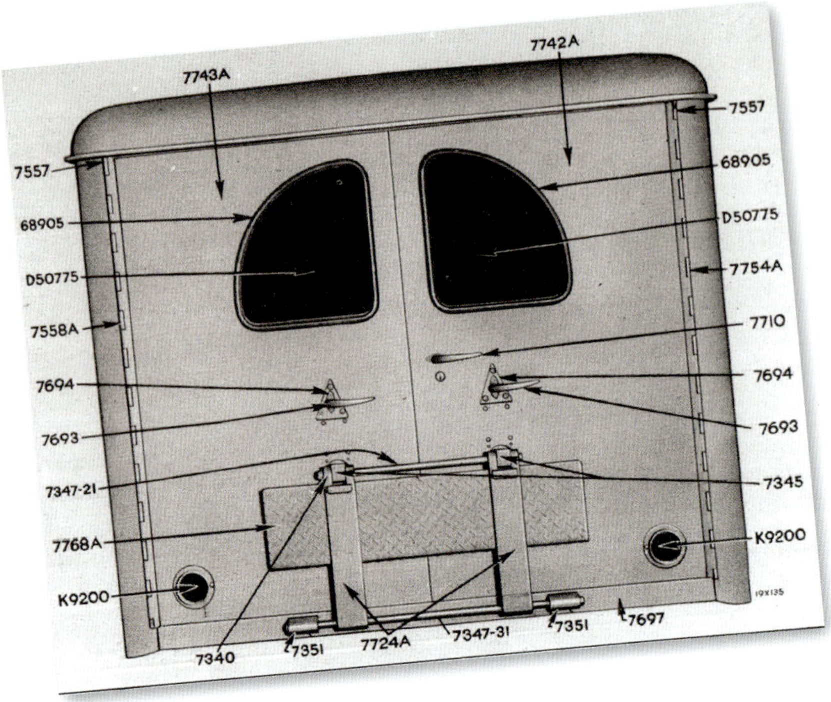

Above: Rear view, doors closed, footstep up.

Below: Rubber shock dampers (D-4300) on the rear doors. Holes for the footstep unlocking handles are just above

Stretcher stop on the rear doors

To prevent the upper stretchers hitting the rear doors during transport, they were equipped with round rubber, then wooden, stops, the latter held in place by two screws.

It is presumed that changing the rubber stops for wooden ones was done after chassis 81625758.

Wooden stops at the bottom of the doors prevented the unfolded stretchers from hitting the doors (7860).

Rear door restraints

The doors were held in place by two scissor arms. They enabled the doors to be locked open in two different positions. When closed, the movement of the doors was dampened by rubber pads on the body.

The locking mechanisms for the doors were protected on the outside by dust screens made of leather or rubber.

Footstep

The rear footstep gave access to the body and could be folded up. When moving, it was held in place by two locks incorporated into the rear door. Locking it up was by means of two independent handles for each lock. Unbolting the step could be done from the inside and from the outside. The handles were turned to the right on the outside.

The shafts comprising the footstep extension system were held sideways by split pins.

In order to dampen the footstep when it was folded, the doors had two black rubber shock dampers (D-4300) on the outside. They were often repainted white when new markings were added.

Above: Windowpane seal on the rear door.

Above center: First type of stretcher stop inside the rear doors.

Above right: England, August 1944. This view shows the right-hand rear door and its fittings (*NARA*)

Below: The rubber stretcher bumper can be seen clearly on the rear door. (*NARA*)

UNITED STATES
ARMY

3 Electrical and Heating Cables

Cable harness

There was a specific harness for the earlier Dodge WC54s and another for the later ones.

The difference between the two was limited to the cabling for the blackout light, which is absent on the early vehicles.

The cables were housed under the hood and were common to other models of six-volt Dodge WCs.

The cable harness consisted of three distinct elements.

References for the earlier vehicles

CC925404: firewall instrument harness.
CC925440: control harness to the firewall terminal.
CC925439: harness connecting the front and rear lights to the firewall terminal.

References for the later vehicles

The later style of harness was installed on chassis 81545122 onwards except for the series 81556098–81553354, and 81556344, 81556349, 81556354, 81856359, and 81556378 (all retained the first style of harness).

CC925405: firewall instrument harness.
CC927105: control harness to the firewall terminal.
CC927104: harness connecting the front and rear lights to the firewall terminal.

Below: Dashboard electrical bundle.

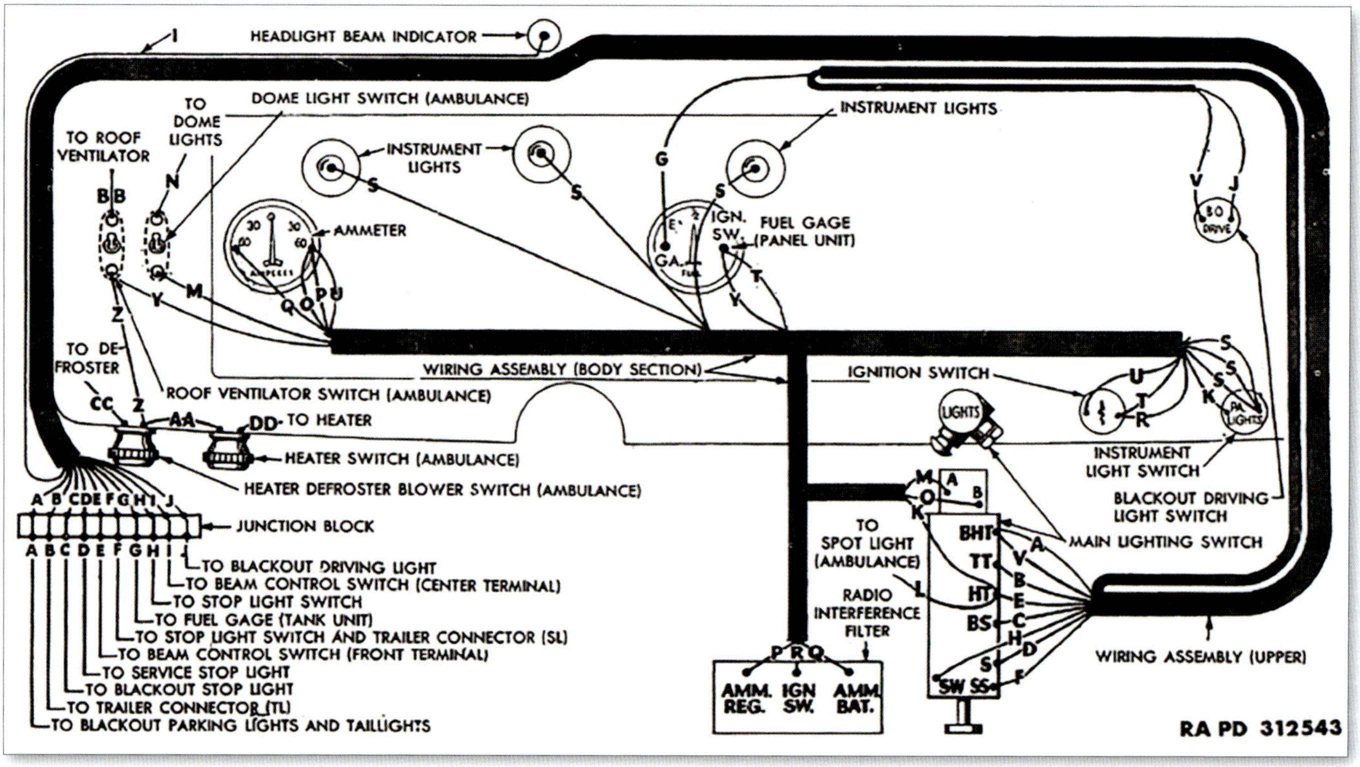

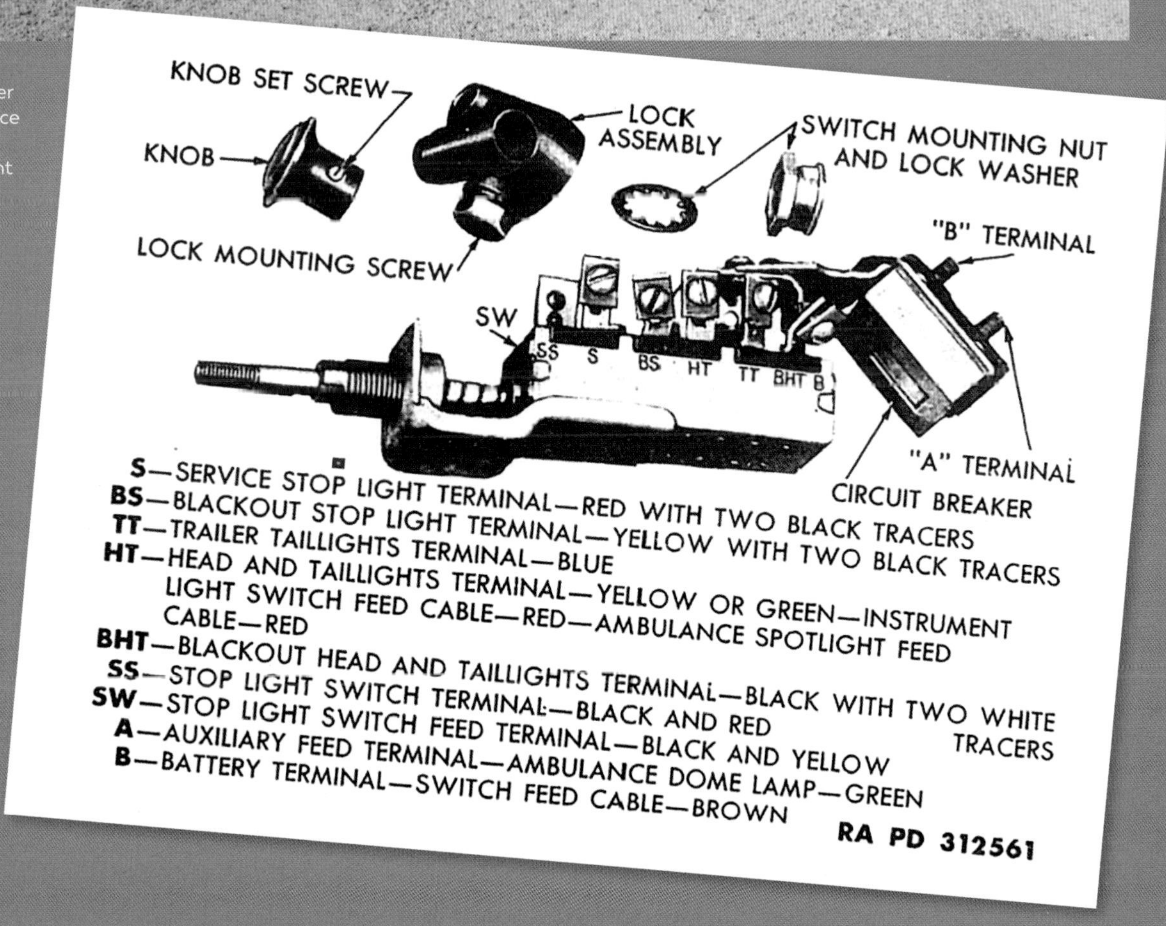

Above: Iran, 12 November 1943. The third ambulance has no blackout light so its radiator and headlight grilles are symmetrical. (*NARA*)

Right: Main "LIGHTS" control. (*TM9-808*)

BONDING (GROUND STRAP)

INTERNAL-EXTERNAL TEETH LOCK WASHERS

Top left: The grommet CC78016 was common to both models. It was located under the dashboard to protect the instrument harness going through the bodywork.

Top and above: Set of serrated washers regularly used on the Dodges.

Left: Most of the Dodge's screws were installed with serrated washers.

Ground strap specific to the ambulance

CC926123 (x 1): ground strap from the steering wheel column to the firewall.

CC923719 (x 1): body to left-hand bumper.
CC926053 (x 1): battery tray to the splash shield.
CC923720 (x 1): firewall to the engine.

Right: CC926123: Ground strap from the steering wheel column to the firewall.

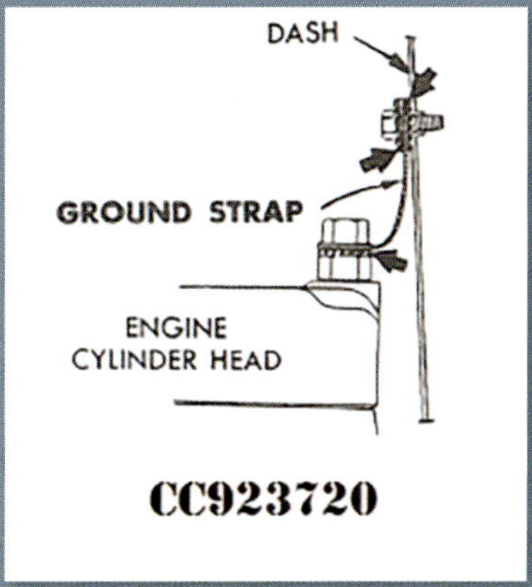

Left and right: CC923720: cylinder head ground strap to the firewall.

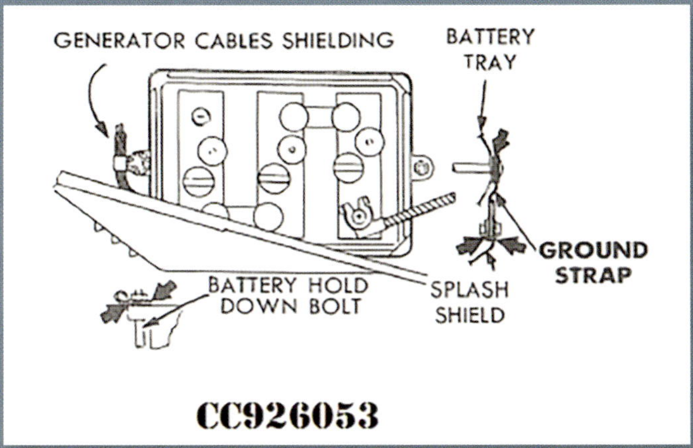

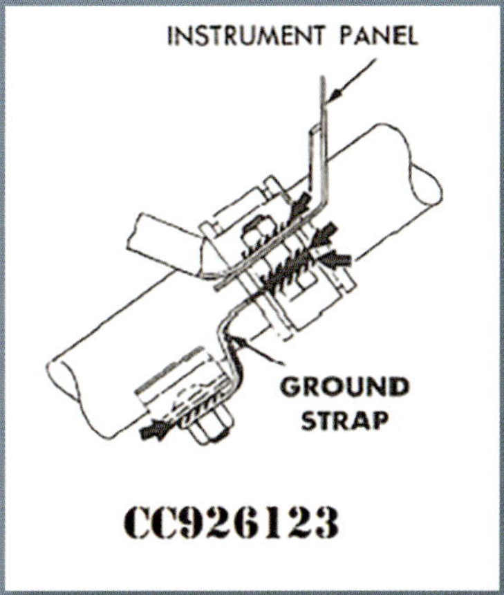

Left: CC926053: battery tray to the splash shield firewall.

Right: CC926123: ground strap from the steering wheel column to the firewall.

Below and inset: CC923719: details of the body ground strap on the left bumper.

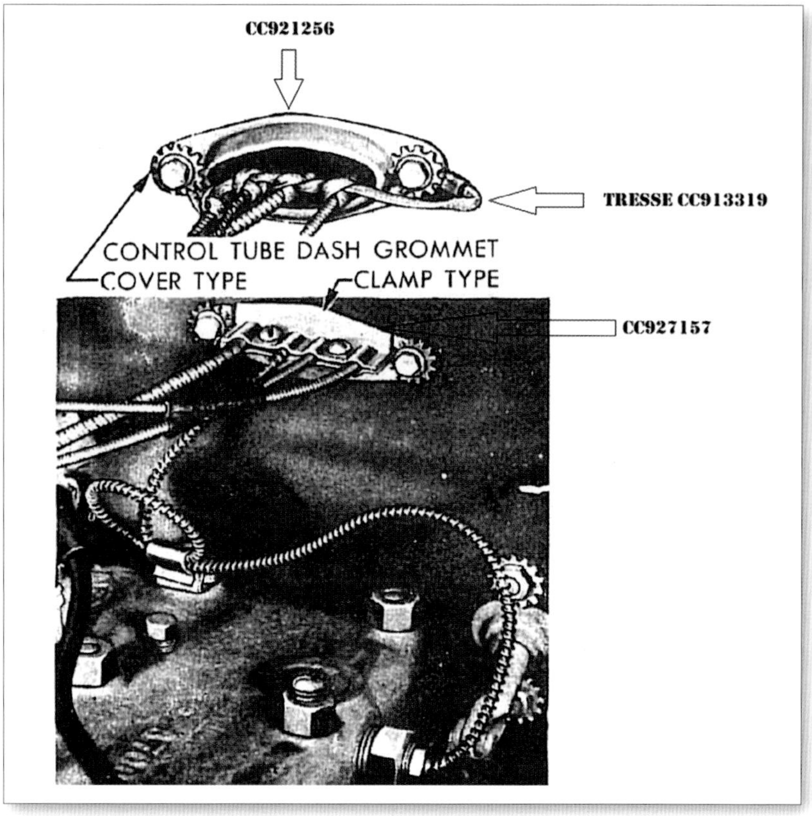

Common ground straps

CC923720 (x 1): front left chassis to the splash shield.
CC922518 (x 1): right hand engine to the chassis.
CC925376 (x 1): left side of engine to the chassis.
CC922537 (x 1): between the steering column and the coil.
CC925385 (x 3) hood ground strap.
CC913319 (x 1) ground strap of the firewall pull tab only up to chassis 81579075, except for the series 8156901–81589513.

Trailer plug

The ambulance was a vehicle that did not have a trailer plug although it was equipped with a hook for towing. The hook was used as a fixed point for pulling in case of breakdown or other unforeseen problems.

Heater and de-icing system

The ambulance was fitted with heating and windshield de-icing equipment so the wounded and the crews could be more comfortable.

The system consisted of a heater made by Tropic Aire, model 16260, installed in the passenger's footwell.

Above: CC913319: ground strap for the firewall cable clamp.
Below: This view of a damaged vehicle shows it is not equipped to tow a trailer. (*Signal Corps*)

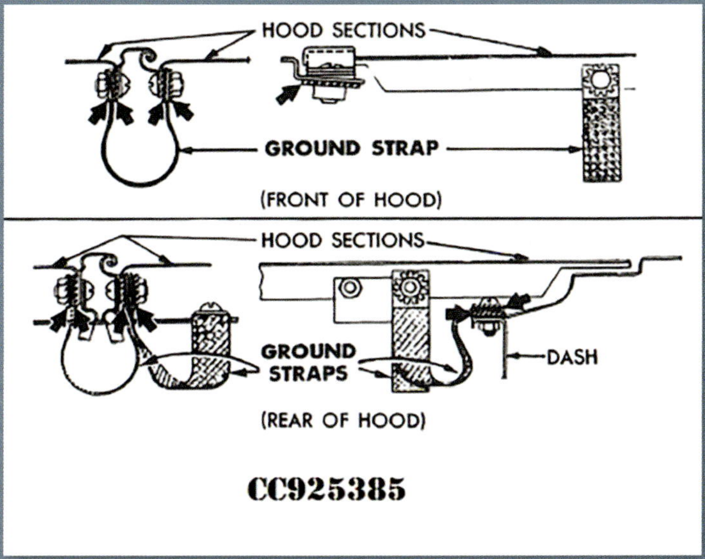

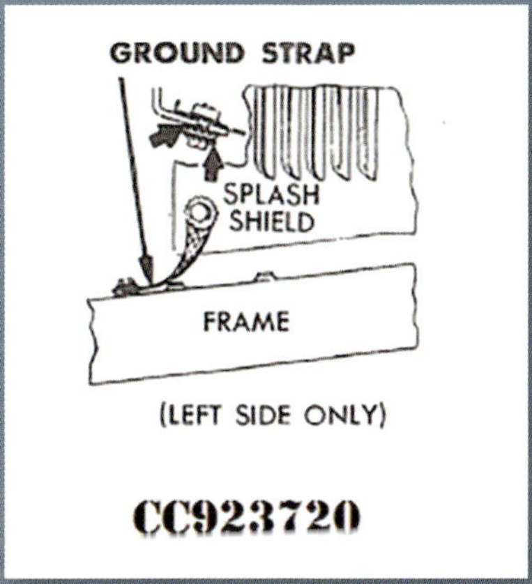

Top left and top right: CC925385: hood ground strap.

Above and above right: CC923720: front left-hand chassis ground strap to the splash shield.

Right: CC922537: ground strap between the steering column and the coil. These usually formed a single strap.

Below right: CC925376: left-hand chassis ground strap.

Below: CC922518: right-hand chassis ground strap.

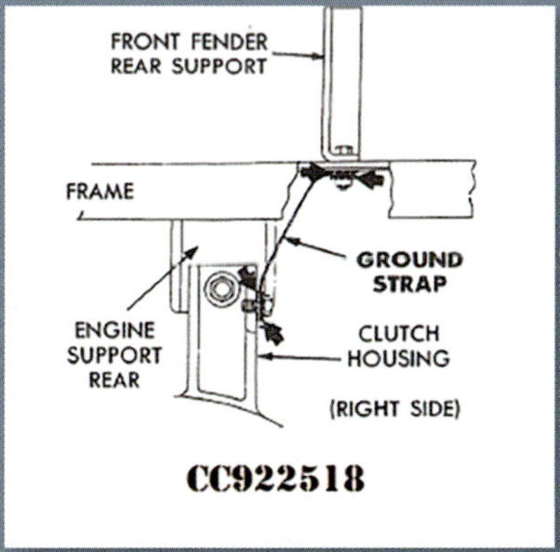

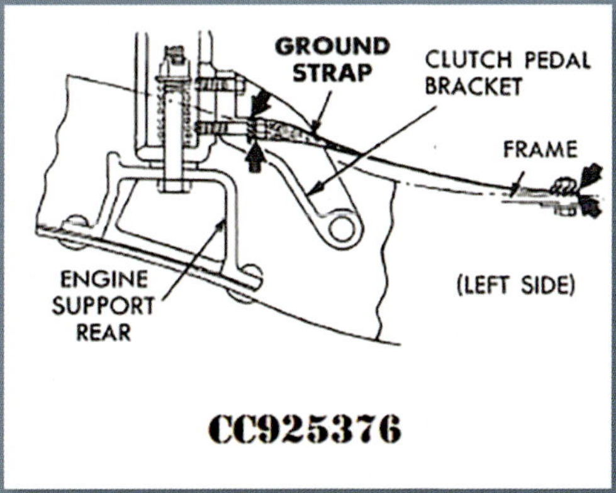

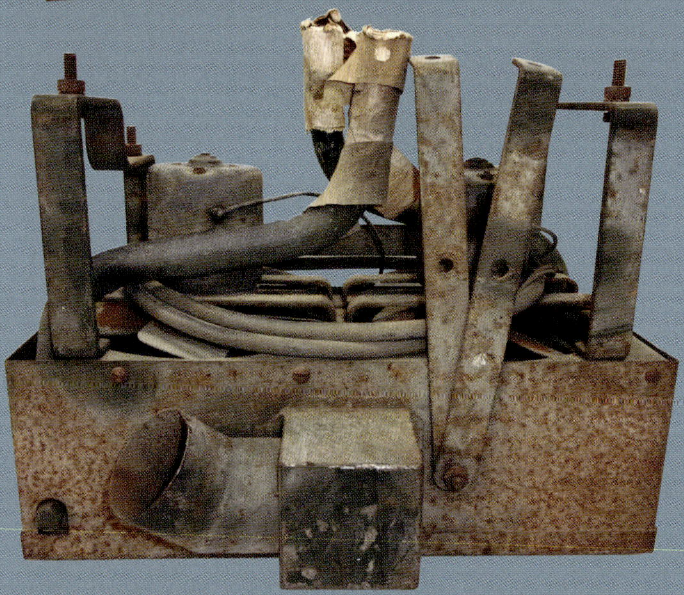

Above: Complete radiator from postwar stock identifiable by its lack of front face plate and the bent upper air outlet.

Left: Cabin heater located in the passenger footwell. The de-icer blower system is visible behind it.

Opposite, top: The heating recess took up part of the passenger floor.

Opposite bottom left: Oval plate designating the model of heater. It is fixed to the rear of the heater on the fan support and held in place by two rivets.

Opposite bottom right: Maker's plate—Tropic Aire.

DETROIT, U.S.A.
DODGE TRUCKS
DIVISION OF CHRYSLER CORPORATION
DETROIT, MICH.
NOMENCLATURE
MODEL SERIAL NO
SUPPLY ARM OR SERVICE MAINTAINING TRUCK
GROSS WEIGHT LBS. MAX.PAYLOAD LBS.
MAX.TRAILED LOAD LBS. DATE DELIVERY
RECOMMENDED OCTANE RATING GASOLINE 70 MIN.
RECOMMENDED S.A.E. GRADE OIL SUMMER—30
RECOMMENDED S.A.E. GRADE OIL WINTER—10
OPEN THE RADIATOR DRAIN COCK-A
AT FRONT LOWER RIGHT HAND
CORNER OF RADIATOR CORE AND THE
CYLINDER BLOCK DRAIN COCK-B AT
THE LOWER LEFT SIDE OF ENGINE.
TROPIC-AIRE

TROPIC-AIRE INCORPORATED
CHICAGO ILL.
MADE IN U.S.A.
IN ALL CORRESPONDENCE REGARDING THIS
HEATER ALWAYS MENTION MODEL NUMBER
MODEL

TROPIC-AIRE

The heat was delivered by two electric fans. The rotation speed of the motors was controlled by a rheostat located to the left of the driver.

The water used by the heater came from the cooling circuit of the engine. The start of the heating circuit was at the firewall end of the cylinder head. It was controlled by a tap (CC947095) which was closed off in hot weather to prevent water circulating to the heating circuit. The return was through a bypass at the front of the engine, above the water pump. The hose was linked to the engine by a right-angled bend (CC926045).

The feeder pipe in the engine compartment was held in place by a collar on the air filtermounting tab (only for Zenith carburetors).

The brass plates marked "Tropic Aire" were on each end of the heater's front.

There were two types of heater bodies. They differed by their upper air outlets. On the postwar type, there was a bend and no attachment holes for the front plates.

De-icing the windshield

The heater casing comprised an upper air outlet. This flow of air into the fan was controlled by an electric motor. The air was then redirected into a steel "Y" and directed onto the windshield to get rid of ice or condensation.

Heating and de-icing controls

These controls were located on the bottom left corner of the firewall. They were two independent rheostats which controlled the de-icing (left) and heating (right).

Below: Cab heating hose collar.

Inset: Installation diagram for the heater. The arrows indicate the use of serrated washers.

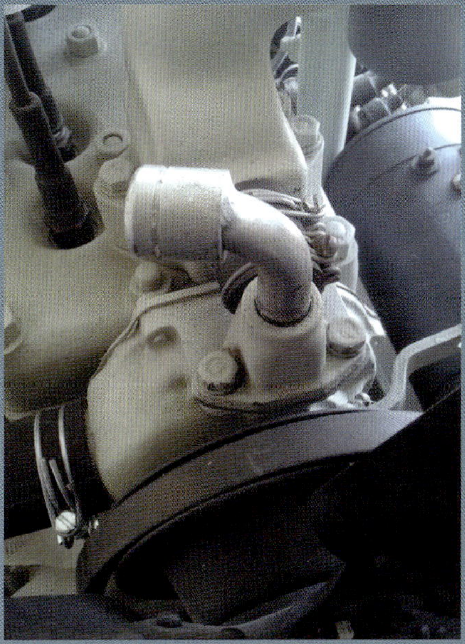

Above: Original model of factory-installed tap.

Above center: Water-return bend of the heating system fitted to the pump bypass.

Above right: Tap found in the packaging carton of a postwar radiator.

Right: Windscreen de-icing vent.

Below: Ventilation system with the "Y" distributor above directing the flow of warm air towards the windshield.

Below right: Heating and de-icing rheostats.

An ambulance from the 111e Bataillon Médical of the 36e Division d'Infanterie in Italy. Its spotlight has been painted with a Red Cross. (*NARA*)

4 Accessories

Spotlight

The spotlight is an Appleton Electric Series 90. It was controlled by a switch on the handle and worked when the "LIGHTS" switch was pulled onto the second position. The handle was also made by Appleton.

The spotlight cable went into the dashboard through a hole the same diameter as the cable. This was connected to the high tension terminal of the main "LIGHTS" switch.

Certain images show a second type of spotlight which is not referenced in the spare parts list. It was probably made by Unity. The Dodge WC64KD was subsequently fitted with two models of spotlights: a Unity model (CC1090541) and a Guide model (GL926662). It must be presumed some WC54 ambulances were fitted with a Unity spotlight as well. This model was distinguished by its arm and handle being different to the Appleton.

The Unity model was certainly fitted on a Dodge registered 733572, photographed on 18 March 1944 at the U.S. Army's Aberdeen Proving Ground, in Maryland, USA. It was part of an order of 3,144 examples—contract W374 ORD 6322—registered USA 732636 to USA 735779. This was the last WC54 order, production running from mid-December 1943 to April 1944.

Beware: the Unity 175-U-I 6 model spotlight, referenced as 6220-733-8879, was often assigned to the Dodge WC54. It was

SPOTLIGHT ASSEMBLY (AMBULANCE)
SERVICED BY APPLETON ELECTRIC,
CHICAGO, ILLINOIS

946953	Door	Appleton Electric No. L-1602	1
946954	Door screw		1
■794088	Lens	Appleton Electric No. 20188	1
■689853	Gasket (lens)	Appleton Electric No. L-1604	1
■689854	Reflector	Appleton Electric No. L-69	1
■689856	Spring (reflector)	Appleton Electric No. L-1537	3
■689857	Spring grip	Appleton Electric No. L-1536	3
■689855	Pressure plate (reflector)	Appleton Electric No. L-1606	1
107403	Bulb (5.25 amp.)		1
■689858	Bulb cap	Appleton Electric No. L-1638	1

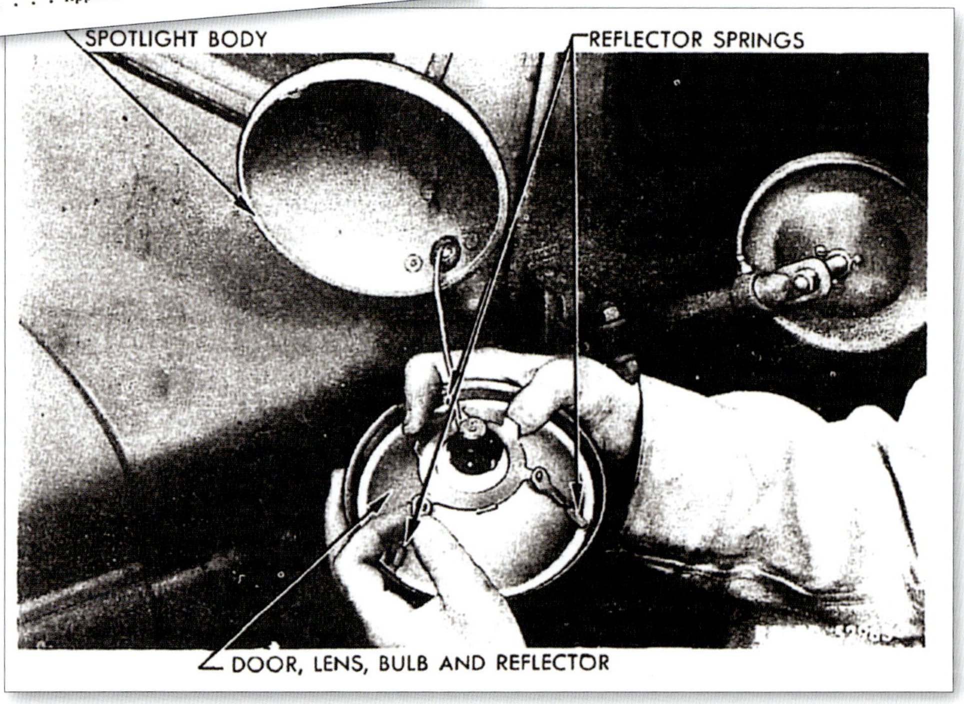

Above: The list of components required to fit and operate the Appleton S90 searchlight. (*SNL G657*)

Right: Installation of searchlight bulb. (*TM9-808*)

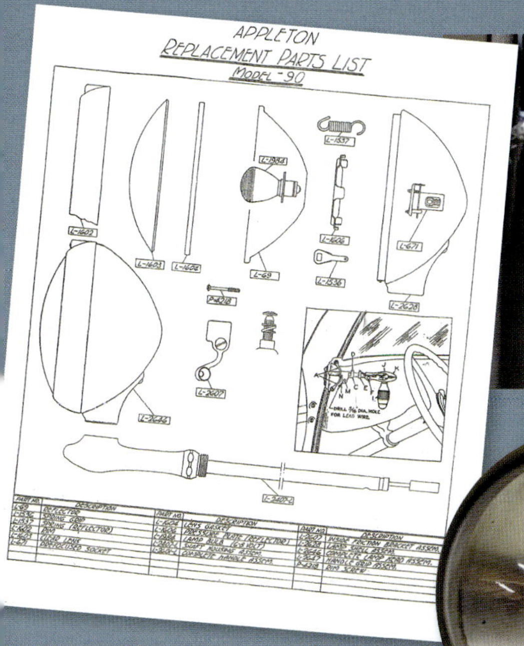

Above: Control handle for the spotlight, this one coming from a range of civilian lights. We can only assume this was originally chromed. It was made by Appleton, just like the light.

Above right and below: Appleton S90 spotlight.

Left:

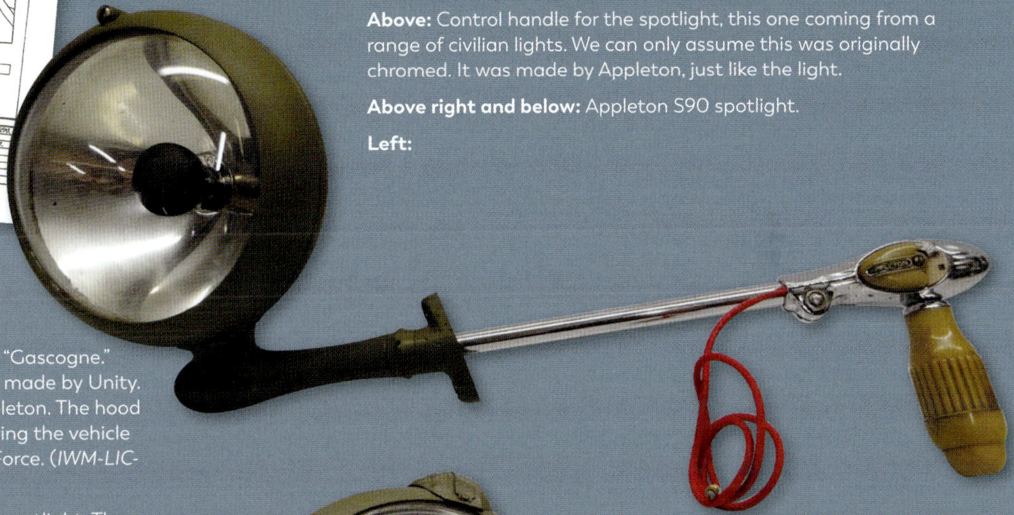

Above: Diagram for the Appleton spotlight.

Bottom right: Jacqueline Becharp, from Lorraine, poses proudly in her ambulance "Gascogne." This was fitted with a spotlight, probably made by Unity. The detail shows it certainlyis not an Appleton. The hood is decorated with a consular flag, identifying the vehicle as being from the French Expeditionary Force. (*IWM-LIC-24990-Z91 3F4*)

Bottom center: The handle for the Unity spotlight. The arm and handle unit was specific to the model and could not be installed with the Appleton version.

Below and bottom left: Unity 56 spotlight.

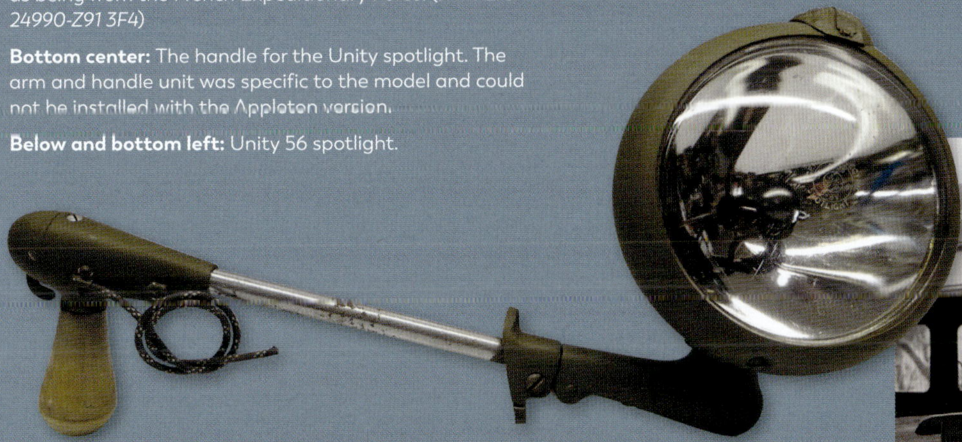

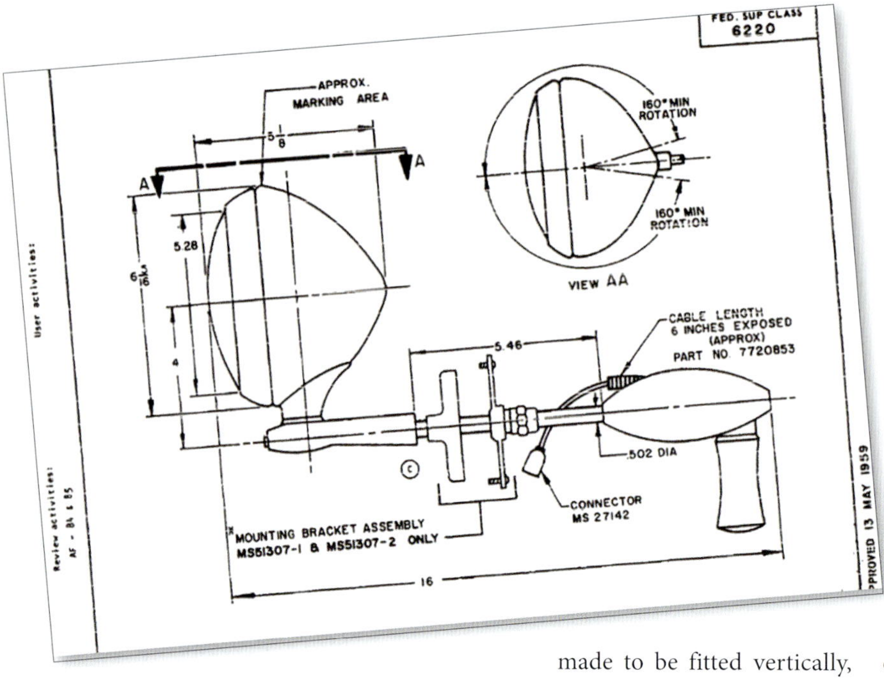

Above: An extract from a Federal Stock diagram concerning a spotlight with, as a reminder at top right, the category classification code "6220."

made to be fitted vertically, i.e., placed on the roof of the vehicle.

This was a development, originally fitted to the GMC M27 Bomb Service truck with the reference G508 73 38879, that also appeared on the Dodge WC64KD ambulance with a reference common to both vehicles: G502 56 07406.

The reference indicated on the plate—6220-733-8879 (see photo below)—is the Federal Stock Number. This coding system was used by the Federal Government from 1955 to 1974. It was conceived to simplify and standardize the catalogue of items the Department of Defense used frequently. It replaced the former jumble of cataloguing systems in use (SNL).

The code "6220" was the prefix to the "Electrical vehicular lights and fixtures" category; the 733-8879 simply recalled the original code (G508 73 38879).

Roof rack

Crews regularly transported items on the roof so as to leave the inside of the vehicle free. The equipment could be placed on the roof itself or on racks.

This assembly was neither regulation nor mass-produced. It was adapted to the situation and made in the field. There are no documents or photos to show how they were made. Each roof rack was unique.

Below: Identification plate of the spotlight with its arm.

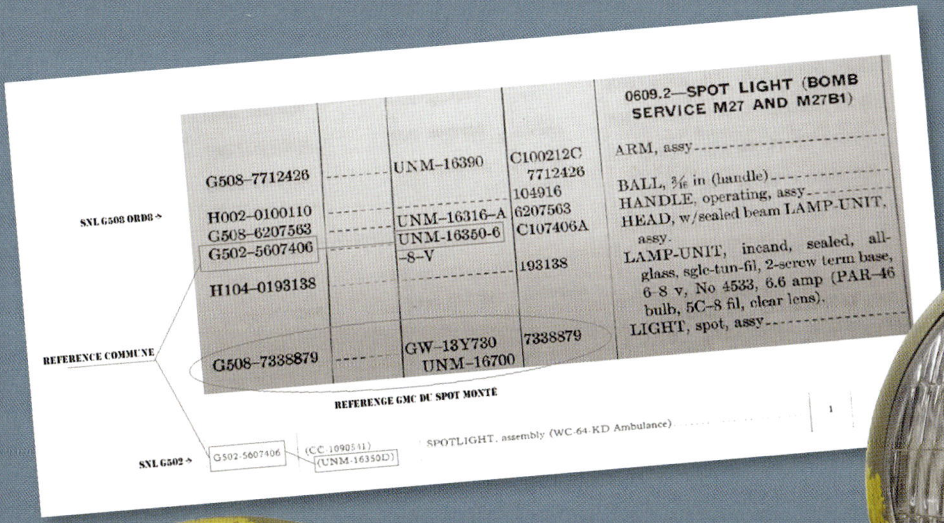

				0609.2—SPOT LIGHT (BOMB SERVICE M27 AND M27B1)
G508-7712426		UNM-16390	C100212C 7712426	ARM, assy
			104916	BALL, 3/16 in (handle)
H002-0100110		UNM-16316-A	6207563	HANDLE, operating, assy
G508-6207563		UNM-16350-6	C107406A	HEAD, w/sealed beam LAMP-UNIT, assy.
G502-5607406		-8-V		
H104-0193138			193138	LAMP-UNIT, incand, sealed, all-glass, sglc-tun-fil, 2-screw term base, 6-8 v, No 4533, 6.6 amp (PAR-46 bulb, 5C-8 fil, clear lens).
G508-7338879		GW-13Y730 UNM-16700	7338879	LIGHT, spot, assy

SNL G508 ORD8 →

REFERENCE COMMUNE

REFERENCE GMC DU SPOT MONTE

SNL G502 →	G502-5607406	(CC-1090541) (UNM-16350D)	SPOTLIGHT, assembly (WC-64-KD Ambulance)	1

Above: Comparative details taken from SNLG502 Dodge and G508 GMC, revealing the common spotlight.

Right: The direction of the lens and the identification plate show it was used vertically.

Left: As the arm was specific to the vertical model, the control handle was not in line with the light, meaning it could not be used horizontally, like on the WC54.

Left: Germany, 1945. An improvised rack on the roof of this ambulance. (*National Library of Scotland*)

Below left: Terracina, Italy, 26 May 1944. An ambulance fitted with a makeshift roof rack driving through a devastated town. (*Signal Corps*)

Below right: Stuttgart, 23 May 1945. An example of a makeshift roof rack made by the crew. It appears to be fastened to the roof by four attachment points. Note also the addition of jerry cans and the painted grille. For some unknown reason, this ambulance has a registration number which is too long. We can presume a "5" has been added by mistake, since registration numbers were never more than six figures. (*Signal Corps*)

Jerry can mounting

The usual location for the jerry can mountings were on the front fenders. The standard mounting was fitted to lay flat with four anchoring points. There was also a mounting which enabled the jerry can to be placed upright, using three flat-iron parts.

Another, less common, set-up is sometimes seen: fitting the mounting on the rear door.

Tool rack

These racks were not present on the first ambulances produced. Some photos show them mounted on the rear door or on the body panel on the driver's side. These were makeshift fittings before the maker standardized them in 1943. The tool rack was eventually mounted on the right-hand-side panel. It was held in place by four screws.

Inside, in order to fill the gap between the molding of the bodywork and the panel, and also to reinforce the attachment, a wooden wedge the same length as the rack was inserted into the gap.

The rack was installed at the beginning of the series. It was cumbersome and not practical because it stuck out from the body towards the front. It was replaced by the standardized shorter model. To hold the tools, the short rack needed three 12-inch straps.

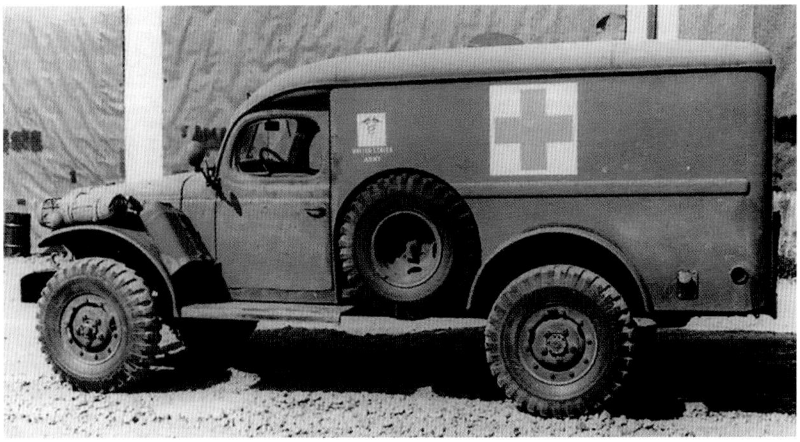

Above left: England, 17 March 1943. Two jerry cans mounted on the fender, not a very common practice. (*Signal Corps*)

Left: Le Muy, southern France, August 1944. The jerry can has been placed upright on the fender, parallel to the movement of the vehicle. Note also the cross painted on the rear windows.

Below left: The jerry can lying flat on the fender. (*NARA*)

Below right: Japan, 12 September 1945. The jerry can has been laid flat on the vehicle fender. (*Signal Corps*)

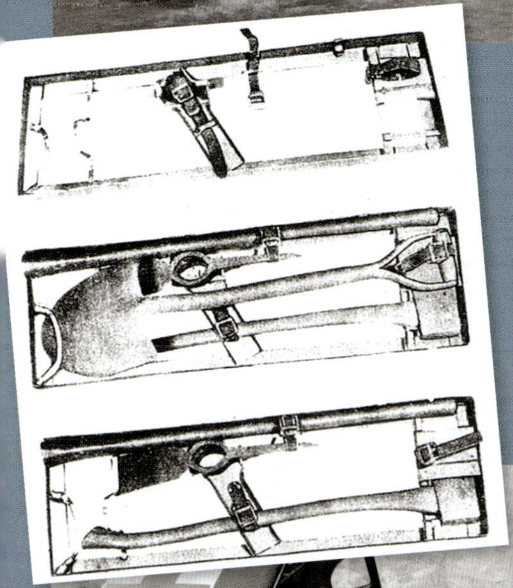

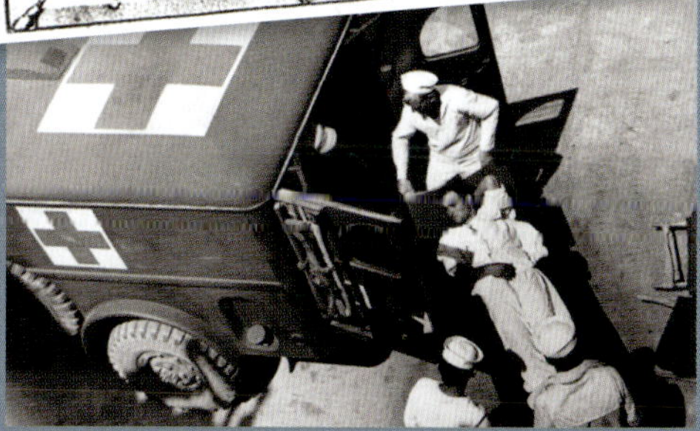

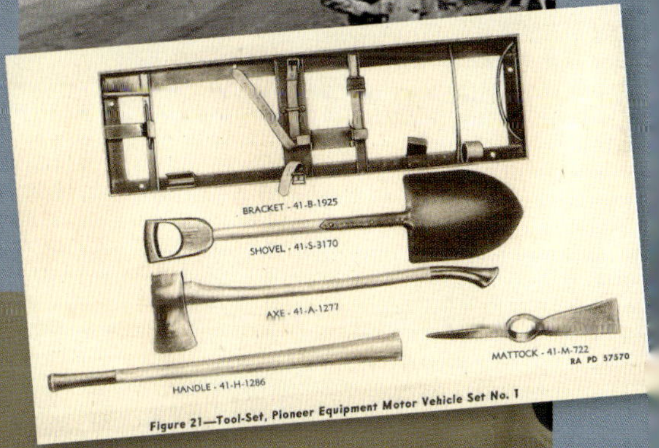

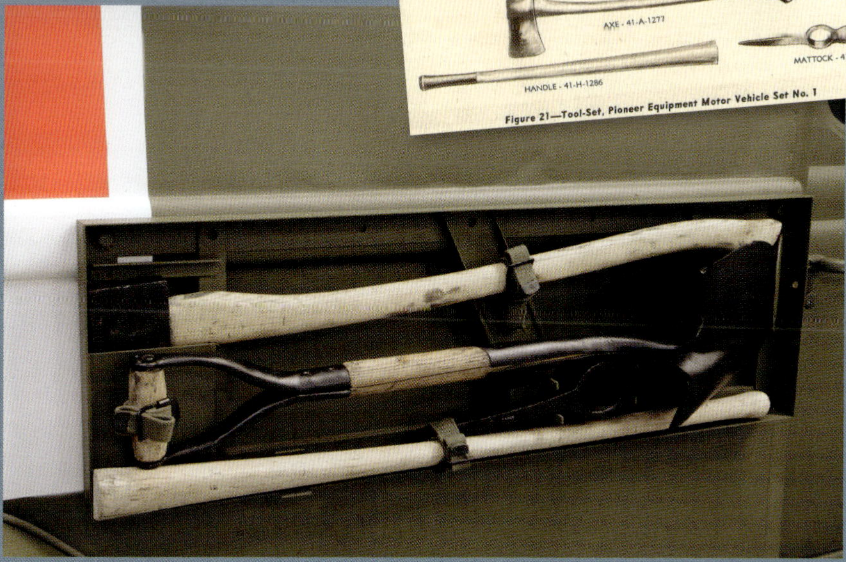

Above left: Le Brenta, Italy, 29 April 1945. A regulation installation for the tool rack. (*Signal Corps*)

Above right: These tool racks have been positioned over the wheel arch. (*NARA*)

Left: The second model of rack, the so-called "short" rack.

Left below: Algeria, July 1943. Italian soldiers, wounded during the invasion of Sicily, are transferred from a ship to WC54 ambulances. The photo shows the tool rack on the rear doors. This practice was common before it was placed on the right-hand panel by the manufacturer. (*Signal Corps*)

Right top: Burma. The absent rack reveals the spacing bar.

Right middle: Rhône Valley, Montélimar sector. This ambulance has the long model tool rack mounted on its rear door.

Right bottom: The so-called "long" model of tool rack.

Below left: Wooden wedge on the panel molding holding the captive nut for the tool rack screws.

Below right: Short model of tool rack in its regulation position.

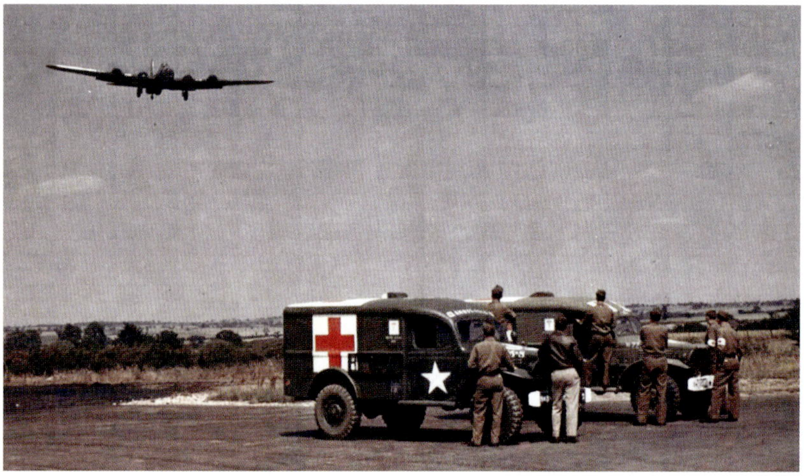

Fire extinguisher and decontaminator

The fire extinguisher was placed in the body on the front right-hand upright. The decontaminator was positioned on the opposite side (on the left). It was held to the panel by six domed metal screws.

Storage box equipment

The boxes housed the equipment and tooling needed to repair the vehicle in case of a breakdown. Most of this equipment was stored in the front right-hand box. The rear of the boxes had a cut-out for holding the arm and leg splints which rested on the s-hook fixed to the inside of the panel.

Splints

The splints were the "armament" of the ambulance. The on-board set consisted of two leg splints (3750000), "Splint, Army, Leg, Half-ring", and two arm splints (3748000), "Splint, Thomas, Arm, Hinged."

Top: England, 1944. The longer tool rack was still *de rigueur* on certain vehicles. A B-17G Flying Fortress of the 381st Bomb Group returns to Ridgewell in Essex. (*NARA*)

Left: The positioning of the tool rack on the rear doors was a regular practice before it was placed on the right-hand panel. (*NARA*)

Below: Constantine, Algeria, 24 May 1943. The decontaminator on the first ambulance is in an unusual position.

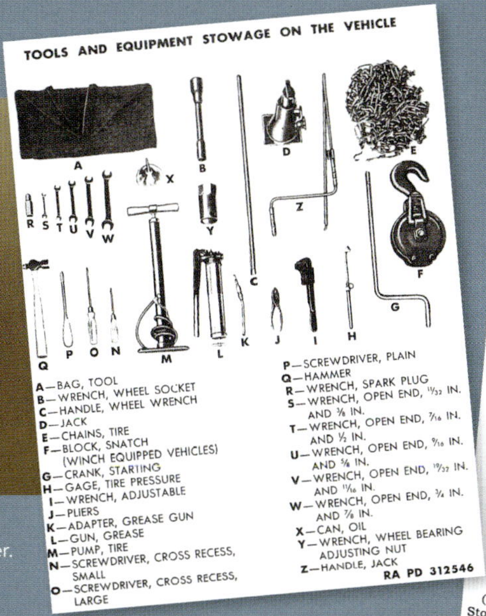

TOOLS AND EQUIPMENT STOWAGE ON THE VEHICLE

A—BAG, TOOL
B—WRENCH, WHEEL SOCKET
C—HANDLE, WHEEL WRENCH
D—JACK
E—CHAINS, TIRE
F—BLOCK, SNATCH (WINCH EQUIPPED VEHICLES)
G—CRANK, STARTING
H—GAGE, TIRE PRESSURE
I—WRENCH, ADJUSTABLE
J—PLIERS
K—ADAPTER, GREASE GUN
L—GUN, GREASE
M—PUMP, TIRE
N—SCREWDRIVER, CROSS RECESS, SMALL
O—SCREWDRIVER, CROSS RECESS, LARGE
P—SCREWDRIVER, PLAIN
Q—HAMMER
R—WRENCH, SPARK PLUG
S—WRENCH, OPEN END, 11/32 IN. AND 3/8 IN.
T—WRENCH, OPEN END, 7/16 IN. AND 1/2 IN.
U—WRENCH, OPEN END, 9/16 IN. AND 5/8 IN.
V—WRENCH, OPEN END, 19/32 IN. AND 11/16 IN.
W—WRENCH, OPEN END, 3/4 IN. AND 7/8 IN.
X—CAN, OIL
Y—WRENCH, WHEEL BEARING ADJUSTING NUT
Z—HANDLE, JACK

RA PD 312546

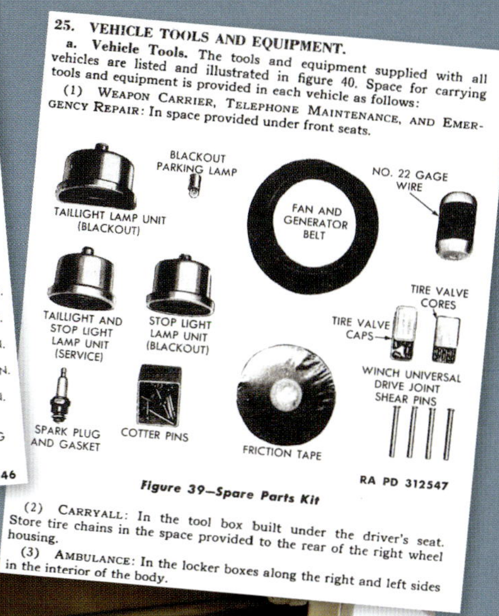

25. VEHICLE TOOLS AND EQUIPMENT.

a. Vehicle Tools. The tools and equipment supplied with all vehicles are listed and illustrated in figure 40. Space for carrying tools and equipment is provided in each vehicle as follows:

(1) WEAPON CARRIER, TELEPHONE MAINTENANCE, AND EMERGENCY REPAIR: In space provided under front seats.

Figure 39—Spare Parts Kit

(2) CARRYALL: In the tool box built under the driver's seat. Store tire chains in the space provided to the rear of the right wheel housing.

(3) AMBULANCE: In the locker boxes along the right and left sides in the interior of the body.

Above left: Production position for the fire extinguisher.

Above center: The vehicle's on-board equipment. (*TM9-808*)

Above right: Spare parts (*TM9-808*)

Right and below: The on-board equipment included two leg splints and two arm splints.

Bottom left: November 1941. A commission examined the first aid equipment needed for ambulances. Here we can see the leg splint 3750000.

Bottom right: Presenting the two types of splints equipping the ambulances. (*National Library of Medicine*)

Spare parts box

The spare parts box (WF-1004-22) was sometimes fixed at the top of the left-hand-side body panel at the front of the vehicle. This installation doesn't seem to have been common practice. Indeed, no SNL manual for Dodges mentions how it was mounted, either for the WC51/52 models or the WC54, whereas for other vehicles equipped with the box—like the Stuart M5, Ward LaFrance and Chaffee—it was duly referenced in the relevant SNLs.

According to the chassis or body numbers referenced, this box appeared at the end of 1943, or the beginning of 1944. It has been noted where it was attached on several models with the body numbers 16673 and 22245 and chassis 81688136. It was installed using a plank fixed between the two uprights of the body with five wood screws.

The box was attached, by means of four captive Tee nuts, to the plank. The shape of the plate and its attachment enabled a solid mounting.

Above: Germany, 21 April 1945. Leg splints can be seen hanging in their place on the inside panel. (*NARA*)

Below: This photo shows the box mounted top left, behind the driver's head.

Left: Spare parts box.

Below left: Wooden wedge mounted on the upright to hold the plate.

Below center: Three specific holes were made on the right-hand upright so they could hold countersunk screws.

Below: Once mounted in place, the plate was subsequently covered by a panel. This example is the original model removed from a vehicle which had not been previously restored. Note also the four holes at top left. Behind these were installed Tee nuts with UNF threads.

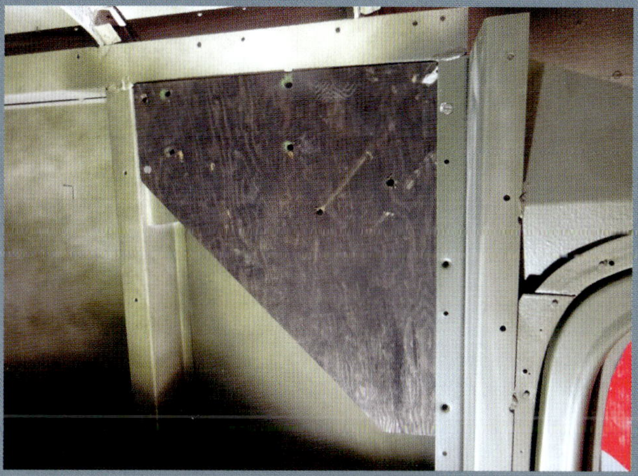

Right: The position of the oil can on the firewall on the left side of the engine compartment.

Oil can

The oil can was mounted above the cab heater feed in the engine compartment.

Flag

In conformity with the Geneva Convention, Article 1, signed in 1864, which protects personnel helping the wounded: "the ambulances and the military hospital are recognized as being neutral and as such, protected and respected by the belligerents." A distinctive sign, a red cross on a white background, enabled personnel helping the wounded to be identified. This was painted on the Dodge WC54 in several places. A flag was often added by the crews in order to make the vehicle even more visible to the enemy. There was no rule for this rather uncommon practice as to where the flag was placed. The most common place was to affix the flag to the radiator grille. It has also been seen on the jerry can mounting with the help of a welded tube.

Fording kit

The fording kit was used to make all the vital systems (air intakes, electricity, etc.) waterproof. It was especially designed to enable the vehicle to move around during amphibious operations like river crossings or beach landings. In order to guarantee air got to the engine without any water, the air filter was removed and replaced by a flexible pipe which went over the vehicle's roof. The electrical parts were sealed to avoid contact with water. The cab was made waterproof by applying a sealing compound to any gaps.

Air and sea transport

When ambulances were shipped by sea from the USA to Europe, the vehicles were prepared with planks and sealing to protect them.

Some vehicles were disassembled, and delivered as parts in crates, to be reassembled on production lines in the field.

Verona, Italy. The standard place for a flag and its pole was on the radiator grille; this ambulance also has the tonnage plate on the grille. (*Signal Corps*)

Right: Rhine, 25 March 1944. The flag has been attached to the grille and carefully furled on its pole. The ambulance has also been painted with a big star for aerial recognition. (*NARA*)

Figure 167—G9-5700769 Kit, Deep Water Fording, Universal, ¼- to 2½-Ton Trucks

A PIPE, flexible metal exhaust, with universal flange, 2 in. I D x 10 ft
B HOSE, ventilating, ¾-in. I D x 10 ft
C CLAMP, air intake hose vent
D PLUG, adapter
E CLAMP, ventilating hose
F HOSE, air intake, wire reinforced flexible rubber, 2½-in. I D x 8 ft
G BUSHING, reducing, 2⅛-in. I D
H BUSHING, reducing, 2¾-in. I D
J WIRE, soft iron, No. 16 gage
K CLAMP, air intake hose
L TOP, air intake hose
M TAPE, non-hygroscopic adhesive
N PAINT, synthetic (Glyptal) red, No. 1201
O COMPOUND, ignition insulation
P GREASE, asbestos
R CEMENT, high temperature
S HOSE, vent, ⅛-in. I D x 6 ft
T TUBING, bundy, ⅛-in. O D
U CLOTH, 18 in square
V BRUSH, flat, varnish
W TECHNICAL MANUAL, TM 9-2853

No. 1 ADAPTER—EXHAUST FLANGE, 2½-Ton GMC
No. 2 ADAPTER—EXHAUST FLANGE, ½-, ¾-, 1½-Ton Dodge
No. 3 ADAPTER—EXHAUST FLANGE, 1½-Ton Chevrolet
No. 4 ADAPTER—EXHAUST FLANGE, ¼-Ton Ford and Willys

No. 1A GASKET, Exhaust, 2½-Ton GMC
No. 2A GASKET, Exhaust, ½-, ¾-, 1½-Ton Dodge
No. 3A GASKET, Exhaust, 1½-Ton Chevrolet
No. 4A GASKET, Exhaust, ¼-Ton Ford and Willys
No. 5A GASKET, Universal Exhaust

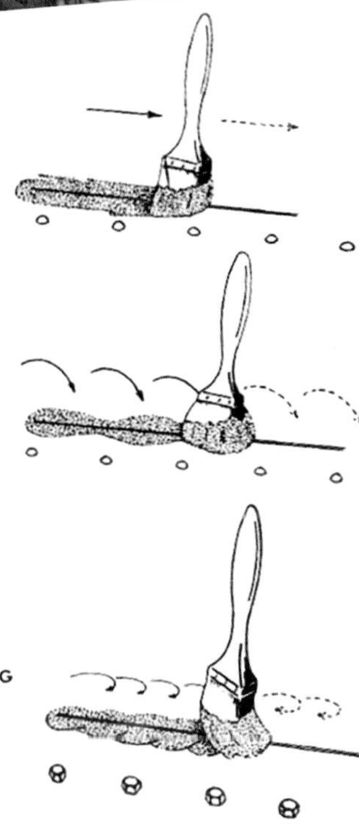

APPLYING
SEALING COMPOUND

DON'T STREAK IT ON,
THIS WON'T FILL THE SEAM

DON'T DAB IT ON EITHER

DO BRUSH FIRMLY WITH A ROTARY MOVEMENT CROSSING THE SEAM. REMEMBER IT IS THE SEAM THAT NEEDS TO BE FILLED WITH SEALING COMPOUND.

RA PD 306199

Figure 1—Applying Sealing Compound

Above left: Fording kit. This kit was suitable for the ¼-ton to 2½-ton vehicle categories.

Above: Instructions for applying the sealing compound to waterproof the unsealed parts of the vehicle.

Left: Sainte-Maxime, 16 August 1944. The driver of the ambulance is removing engine grease from the fording kit following a landing the day before. Note the hole in the hood enabling an air intake pipe to pass through to the carburetor, which meant the air filter was removed. (*NARA*)

Siren

There were no sirens on Dodge WC54 ambulances. To date, despite the hundreds of photographs examined, a siren, mounted on a fender or elsewhere, has never been seen. No documentation or technical nomenclature mentions one being mounted. It is nonetheless possible some enterprising crews could have attached a siren.

Left: India, April 1944. Air and sea transport. Ambulances were disassembled so they could be transported by air to distant or difficult-to-access territories. A recognition star has been painted on the rear doors.

Below: Normandy, 1 July 1944. The three Dodges coming out of the landing craft are equipped with an air intake pipe. Note also that the windshield has been sealed. This means the vehicle has been entirely prepared for a landing in deep water fording conditions. The shipping marking has been applied to the windshield from the inside, certainly on paper. The position of the second vehicle shows a white star on the roof, most likely 25" in diameter, for aerial identification together with a splash on the hood corresponding to gas detection paint. (*NARA*)

Above: 15 August 1944, a landing in the South of France. The first vehicle has a white star on the roof. Note that it is equipped with the fording kit and the tool rack is on the driver's side. (*US Navy*)

Right: Embarking at a North African port in preparation for the landings in Sicily. Makeshift jerry can mounting and fording kit fitted. (*US Coast Guard*)

Left: A Dodge ready for sea transport. These women wear the U.S. Ports of Embarkation insignia and are getting the vehicle ready for delivery. The Ports of Embarkation were set up and exploited by the Transportation Corps to ensure a regular flow of supplies through port installations. The embarkation port was under military command, being responsible for dispatching, transit, storage, and managing other installations often within the geographic limits of the port town. At the end of World War II, the Transport Corps used ports of Boston, New York, Hampton Roads, Charleston, New Orleans, Los Angeles, San Francisco, and Seattle. More than seven million passengers and 126 million tons of goods went through the ports during the war. (*Signal Corps*)

NATIONAL ROAD

Philippines, 28 November 1944. The hood is flatter than on other models. Note the chains on the tires. (*NARA*)

5 Markings and Identification

Regulation markings

Markings were standardized by "Army Regulation 850-5." All official and regulation markings were included for each vehicle.

Over time markings evolved and each unit adapted its markings according to their theater of operations. Per the January 1944 directives, it was planned for ETO (European Theater of Operations) vehicles to have a white star on the roof, this being suppressed in June 1944. Regulation-wise, there were no stars on the doors or on the hood. The stars could be in a circle or not depending on the campaign; these were obligatory markings. The size varied between 25 and 36 inches.

1942

- Side red cross: 18 inches across, 6 inches thick on a 20½-inch white background.
- Rear doors red cross: 8 inches across, 2.6 inches thick on a 10-inch white background.
- Roof red cross: 15 inches across, 5 inches thick on a 47-inch white background
- Above the windshield: two red crosses 3 inches across and 1 inch thick on a 4-inch white background separated by a 28-inch gap with "AMBULANCE" in the center in 3-inch-high letters.
- On each side, a 6-inch caduceus (symbol of medicine) on a white background, 7 inches wide by 7½ inches high.

Right: Original marking on a front door. (*Author's photo*)

Below: Italy, 20 September 1943: circled stars were an unusual design for the time. (*NARA*)

Above: Arkansas, September 1943. Standard small markings. (*Signal Corps*)

Left: Saint-Raphaël, France, 15 August 1944. A 36th Infantry Division ambulance. Despite the poor quality, the door star is still clearly visible. (*NARA*)

Right: 9 April 1943. An ambulance, wearing standard early markings, on stand-by at an aerodrome. (*NARA*)

Left: Sainte-Maxime, 15 August 1944. An ambulance from the 389th Medical Collecting Company. We can see the circled stars on the door and the roof. Strangely, the radiator grill is covered despite the August heat in the South of France. (*NARA*)

Below: India. The standard early style of markings. (*NARA*)

Above: 8th Evacuation Hospital, Teano sector, Italy, 1944. Another example of small markings on a vehicle with a big fuel filler. (*National Library of Medicine*)

Above left: Australia, December 1943. Early medical markings with the second type of fuel filler. The markings do not make sense in helping with identification, but are usually associated with the date of receipt by the U.S. Army. (*NARA*)

Left: An ambulance ready on a landing strip on Makin Island in the Pacific. (*Medical Department—USAAF*)

Below: Wounded arriving by rail en route to Baxter Hospital in Arkansas in 1943. Note the homogeneity of the vehicles which remained in the USA. (Author)

Above: England, 13 May 1944. Markings per the ETOUSA directive are seen on this group of ambulances of the 379th Bomb Group. (*NARA*)

Above inset: England, January 1944. An ambulance follows a 379th Bomb Group B-17 Flying Fortress which has signaled it has casualties on board. The ambulance is wearing the new markings. (*NARA*)

Right: Extract from the Ordnance Motor Vehicles file explaining the markings of the ETOUSA directive.

Below: An Eighth Air Force base, England, March 1944. (*NARA*)

Below right: Harville, France, October 1944. Unfortunately, the red cross has not been respected in this case and appears to have been used as a target. The markings are as per the ETOUSA directive. (*Signal Corps*)

Bottom right: Diagram explaining "XXI-A," the reference of the directive.

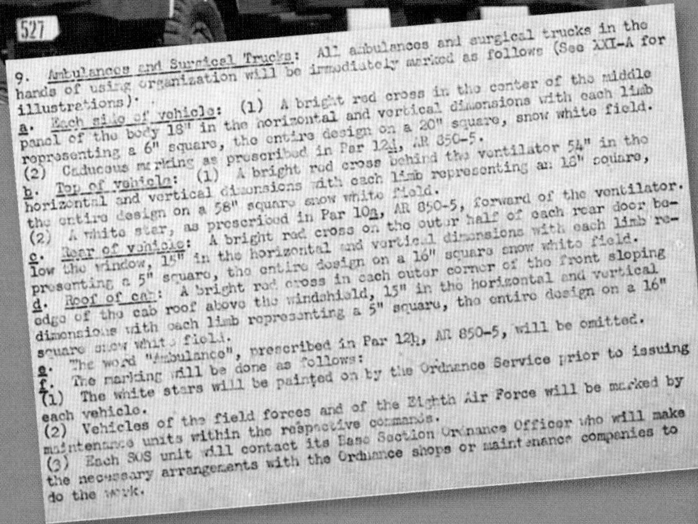

9. Ambulances and Surgical Trucks: All ambulances and surgical trucks in the hands of using organization will be immediately marked as follows (See XXI-A for illustrations).
a. Each side of vehicle: (1) A bright red cross in the center of the middle panel of the body 18" in the horizontal and vertical dimensions with each limb representing a 6" square, the entire design on a 20" square, snow white field.
(2) Caduceus marking as prescribed in Par 12d, AR 850-5.
b. Top of vehicle: (1) A bright red cross behind the ventilator 54" in the horizontal and vertical dimensions with each limb representing an 18" square, the entire design on a 58" square snow white field.
(2) A white star, as prescribed in Par 10a, AR 850-5, forward of the ventilator.
c. Rear of vehicle: A bright red cross on the outer half of each rear door below the window, 15" in the horizontal and vertical dimensions with each limb representing a 5" square, the entire design on a 16" square snow white field.
d. Roof of cab: A bright red cross in each outer corner of the front sloping edge of the cab roof above the windshield, 15" in the horizontal and vertical dimensions with each limb representing a 5" square, the entire design on a 16" square snow white field.
e. The word "Ambulance", prescribed in Par 12h, AR 850-5, will be omitted.
f. The marking will be done as follows:
(1) The white stars will be painted on by the Ordnance Service prior to issuing each vehicle.
(2) Vehicles of the field forces and of the Eighth Air Force will be marked by maintenance units within the respective commands.
(3) Each SOS unit will contact its Base Section Ordnance Officer who will make the necessary arrangements with the Ordnance shops or maintenance companies to do the work.

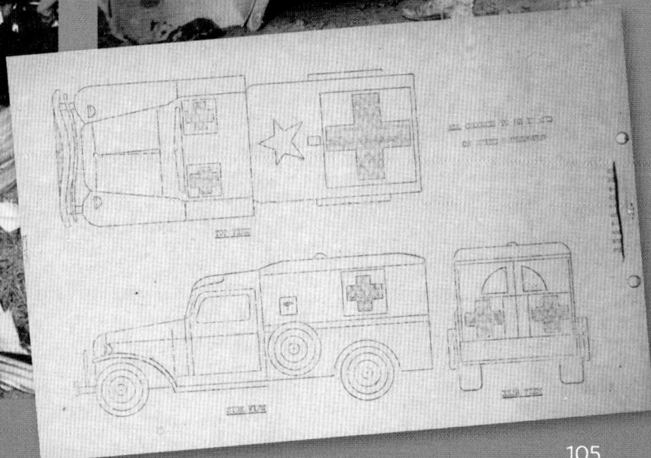

End of 1943–beginning of 1944

According to a directive of the European Theater of Operations, United States Army (ETOUSA), publication of which is thought to have been at the end of 1943 and the beginning of 1944, temporary markings were described with the following characteristics:

All ambulances and surgical trucks in the hands of using organization will be immediately marked as follows (See XXI-A for illustrations).

1. Each side of vehicle: (1) A bright red cross in the center of the middle panel of the body 18″ in the horizontal and vertical dimensions with each limb representing a 6″ square, the entire design on a 20″ square, snow white field. (2) Cadudeus marking as prescribed in Par 12d, AR 850-5.
2. Top of vehicle: (1) A bright red cross behind the ventilator 54″ in the horizontal and vertical dimensions with each limb representing an 18″ square, the entire design on a 58″ square snow white field.
3. Rear of vehicle: A bright red cross on the outer half of each rear door below the window, 15″ in the horizontal and vertical dimensions with each limb representing a 5″ square, the entire design on a 16″ square snow white field.
4. Roof of cab: A bright red cross in each outer corner of the front sloping edge of the cab roof above the windshield, 15″ in the horizontal and vertical dimensions with each limb representing a 5″ square, the entire design on a 16″ square snow white field.
5. The word "Ambulance", prescribed in Par 12b, AR 850-5, will be omitted.
6. The marking will be done as follows:
   a. The white stars will be painted on by the Ordnance Service prior to issuing each vehicle.
   b. Vehicles of the field forces and of the Eighth Air Force will be marked by maintenance units within the respective commands.
   c. Each SOS unit will contact its Base Sanction Ordnance Officer who will make the necessary arrangements with the Ordance shops or maintenance companies to do the work.
7. Materials necessary for marking vehicles as herein prescribed will be obtained from the CG, SCS, ETOUSA (Ordnance Service) excepting paint, liquid vesicant detector, M5, which is obtained from CWS through normal supply channels.

1944–1945

- Side red cross: 33 inches across, 11 inches thick on a 36-inch white background.
- Rear doors red cross: 45 inches across, 15 inches thick on a 47-inch white background.

Opposite top left and right: England. These ambulances are in transition with only the "Ambulance" marking so far replaced by crosses as per the directive. (*NARA*)

Above: The 8th Evacuation Hospital at Pietramala, north of Florence, Italy. The vehicles have the TQM "bar" code and the company indicator "K", identical to the vehicle recently restored. (*National Library of Medicine*)

Above inset: Nordhausen Concentration Camp, April 1945. The ambulance has been given new markings in the field since the reflector is partly painted and the window seal has been painted entirely white. (*Signal Corps*)

Right: Yeron River, Jarny, France, 1944. (*NARA*)

Below: An ambulance of the 82nd Medical Battalion of the 12th Armored Division. Mud flaps are an interesting addition to the fender. The Dodge has been given new markings by sacrificing part of the reflectors. (*National Library of Scotland—The Portal to Texas History*)

Below, right: Nancy, France, 5 November 1944. This ambulance has been given the new markings with the appearance of the red crosses replacing the word "Ambulance." The tool rack was not removed when the new markings were applied. Note also the addition of a star on the door. (*NARA*)

Below: March 1944, Italy. These ambulances, assigned to Ninth Air Force airfield, have received the new forward markings. (*NARA*)

Bottom: Italy, 1944–1945. These markings have just been applied. Overspray has clearly spilled over the masking tape. Moreover, there are no unit markings or registration numbers. All that is left is the TQM code and the company letter "K." (*Signal Corps*)

- Roof red cross: 60 inches across, 20 inches thick on a 60-inch white background
- Above the windshield: two red crosses 3 inches across and 1 inch thick on a 4-inch white background separated by a 28-inch gap with "AMBULANCE" in the center in 3-inch-high letters.
- On each side, a 6-inch caduceus on a white background 7 inches wide by 7½ inches.

Mid-1944–end of 1945

The word "Ambulance" started disappearing, leaving the two Red Crosses.

The caduceus on the sides became round at the very end of the conflict with the inscription "US Army Medical Department" on the inside of the white circle.

Caduceus

There were two types of this marking.

- The rectangular 6-inch version on a white background 7 inches wide by 7½ inches high. The caduceus was simplified, the wings not being detailed.
- The round version was inside a white 10-inch diameter circle. The caduceus measured 7¾ inches high by 6½ inches wide. It was more elaborate and bore the inscription "US Army Medical Department" in the white section.

Regulation positioning of the Red Crosses

The caduceus on the forward end of the body panel was positioned five inches from the front metal joint and seven inches from the roof gutter.

The white background of the roof Red Cross was initially positioned at the rear limit of the roof ventilation.

The first model of Red Cross on the sides was centered on the panel.

The front "leg" of the later roof Red Cross was positioned at the front limit of the roof ventilation.

Above: England, 1944. This medical convoy is waiting for the possible evacuation of patients arriving by plane. The ambulance features the latest type of markings. (*Medical Department—USAAF*)

Right: England, 18 January 1944. Large crosses of the last type of markings have been applied to the forward roof of the ambulance, whereas the side cross has kept its first-generation dimensions. (*NARA*)

Below right: Tacoma, Washington, USA. These ambulances are waiting for wounded to disembark. Note how uniform the markings are with the new round model of caduceus and the appearance of the first 64KD ambulances equipped with blankets. (*ACME*)

Top right and below: India. A correctly shaped caduceus in the right position. (*NARA*)

England, May 1945. The front has been given its new, so-called "end-of-war" markings. (*NARA*)

It could be close to, or far from, the edge of the recess of the spare wheel. The white background stopped under the roof gutter. It was also possible to see the white painted on and over the gutter. This usually happened when new markings were applied.

The second style of side Red Cross was off-center on the panel because of its size and the spare wheel recess. Its horizontal position was not specified precisely.

Applying the markings

Here is a simple, modern technique for applying markings. The stencils were made on request by Ordnance Militaria, a company specializing in the design of customized stencils (www.ordmilitaria.com).

The following tones are recommended: white RAL 9016 and red RAL 3000.

Painted windows

Depending on the theater of operations, the rear windows were partly, or even wholly, painted over.

APPLYING THE CADUCEUS

1. Position the stencil with the help of sticky tape.
2. Remove part of the backing paper and stick that part of the stencil, smooth it down with the help of a flat spatula, then do the same with the other part.
3. The stencil is now correctly applied.
4. In order to prevent overspray, protect the rest of the vehicle.
5. You can use a spray can or a spray gun. Apply the paint lightly without seeking full coverage on the first pass.
6. Remove the stencil delicately after allowing the paint to properly dry.
7. When the white background is dry, position the stencil of the caduceus in the same manner as above.
8. Apply a thin layer of red. It may appear light but will darken as it dries.

APPLYING THE "AMBULANCE" MARKING

1. When the stencil is delivered in one piece, the ambulance markings and the crosses are aligned along its bottom. In order to correspond to the original markings of the photograph on pages 118–119, the following modification must be made: find and mark the vertical center of the white background of the cross as well as that of the word "Ambulance." Next, cut the stencil into three parts.
2. Find and mark the center of the word "Ambulance" in order to position it correctly on the vehicle.
3. Align your centering marks.
4. The center of the word "Ambulance" must be placed on the fold of the roof. The vertical position of the stencil is found by its relation to the body joint strip. The bottom of the word "Ambulance" is positioned four inches from this.
5. Apply the stencils as per the techniques explained above.
6. Application of the stencils for the Red Crosses is done in the same way as for the caducei.

Applying the caduceus

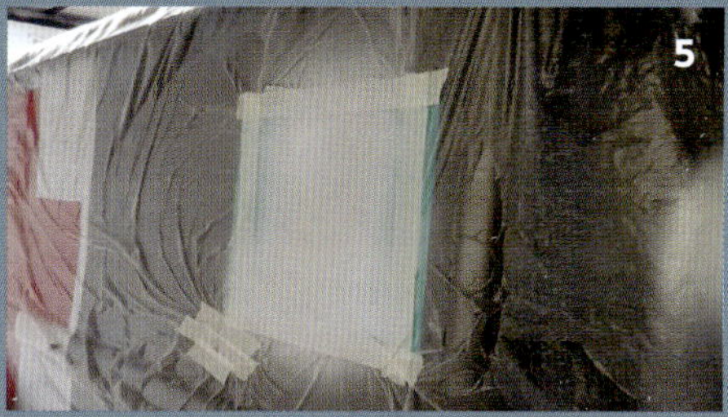

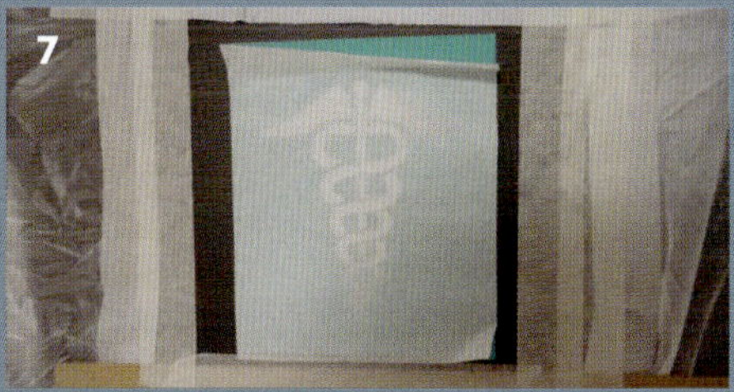

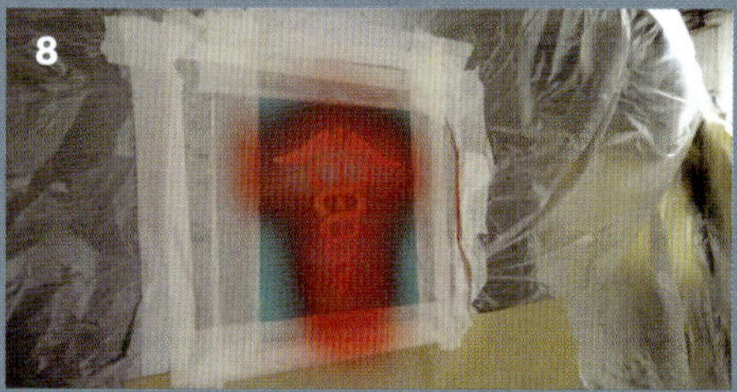

Applying the "Ambulance" marking

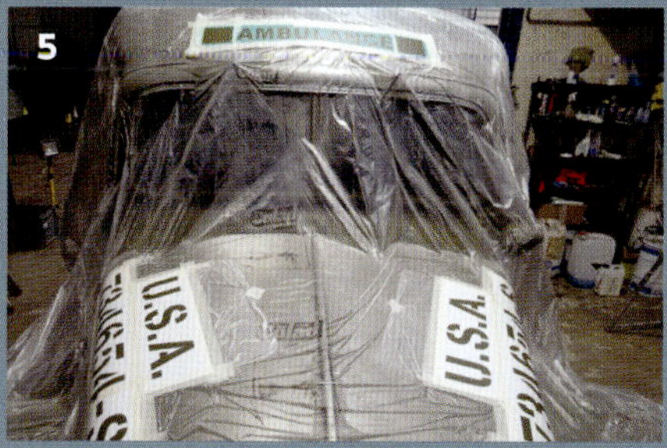

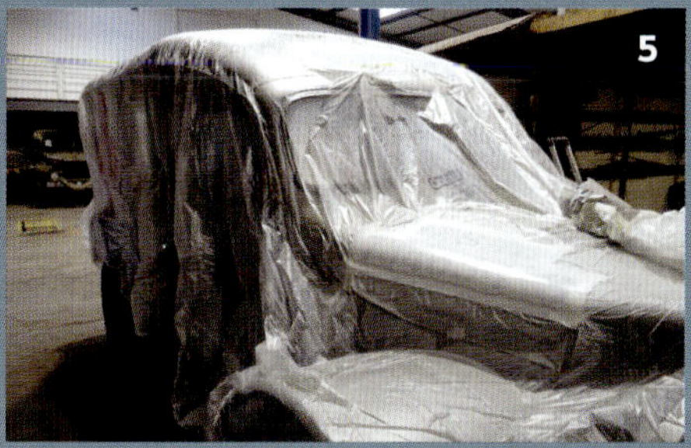

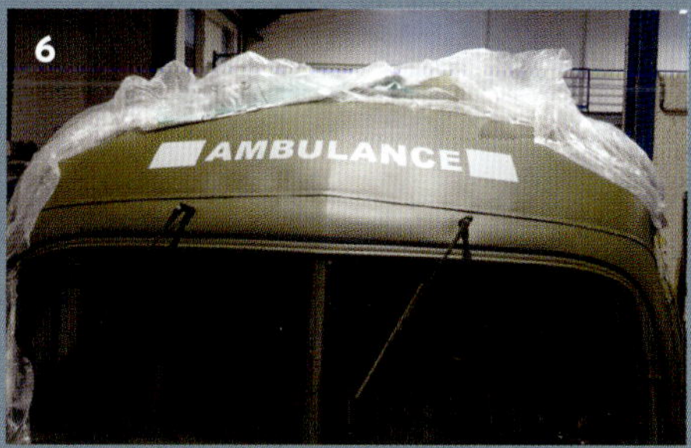

White background on the roof

Some vehicles had a bigger than usual white background on the roof. This was common practice in the American Field Service.

Registration numbers

The registration number consisted of at least five digits, with a maximum of six, depending on the year of production. The number started with a "7."

Above: Futa Pass, Italy. Only the red cross has been painted on the rear windows. (*NARA*)

Right: 500th Bomb Group, Saipan, Mariana Islands. An example of the hood registration number. (*NARA*)

Below: San Pietro, Italy. The rear window is partly covered by the cross. This was common practice. (*Signal Corps*)

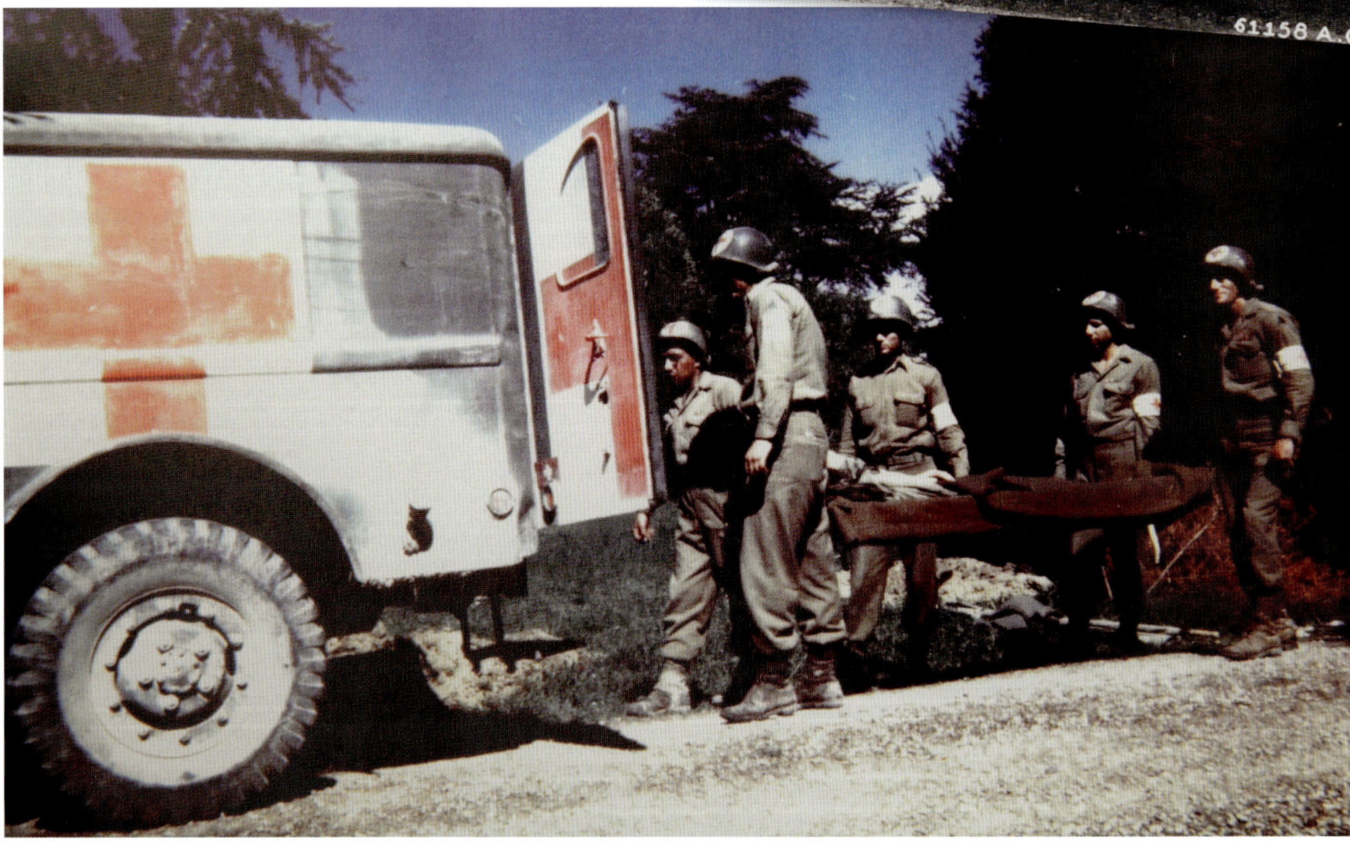

Above: England, summer 1944. The rear window was partly painted over when the new markings were applied. (*Signal Corps*)

Left: Nettuno, Italy, March 1944. The roof marking covers the entire rear section of the roof. Note the jerry can mount fixed to the door. (*ACME*)

Right: Southern France, 15 August 1944. The white paint on the roof extends right to the edge. The vehicle is fitted with a fording kit. (*Signal Corps*)

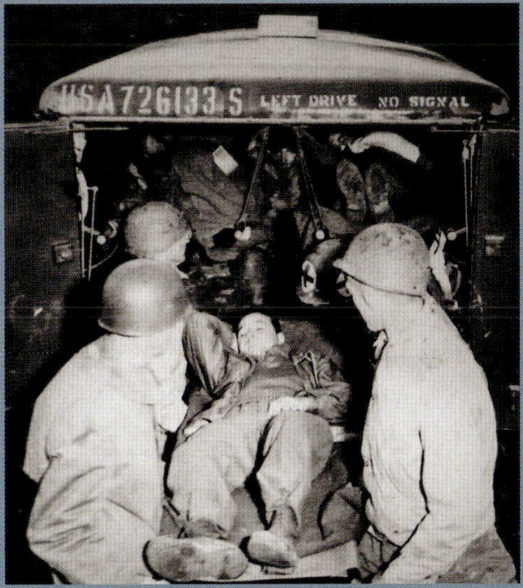

Bottom left: France, 24 September 1944. Registration markings followed by the radio interference suppression "S" marking as well as the left-hand-drive warning. These suggest the vehicle had transited via England. (*Signal Corps*)

Bottom right: The ambulance's registration number followed by the suppression "S" can be seen here. (*National Library of Medicine*)

The last WC54 taken on charge by the U.S. Army in April 1944 was 735779.

Receipt registration numbers were painted in blue from 1942. They were two inches tall and preceded by "USA."

From 1944 onwards, white four-inch markings were applied over the blue markings following a directive from the American Forces Command in Great Britain. The number could be followed by the letter "S" indicating the vehicle had a suppressor (to eliminate radio interference caused by its electrical system).

Shipping marking

The shipping marking was a summary of the vehicle's dimensions, weight and volume used for sending vehicles by sea. It was to be found at the bottom of the right-hand-side body panel, under the tool rack. It could be preceded by: "From US PORT AGENCY WAR SHIPPING ADM NY."

WEIGHT	5920 LBS.
LENGTH	194.50 IN.
WIDTH	77 IN.
HEIGHT	90 IN.
VOL	791 CU.FT.

Tonnage classification

From 1943 onwards, the vehicles were classified with a tonnage indicator.

This vehicle classification enabled bridges to be marked with the class of vehicles that could cross them without risk. The ambulance was in the fourth class. The indicative "4" was painted in black on a yellow background on a plate hooked to the radiator grille or the vehicle fender or painted directly on the bodywork.

France, 20 August 1944. The shipping marking can just be seen under the tool rack. (*Signal Corps*)

Above: England, 19 June 1944. The shipping marking is clearly visible under the tool rack. Note the edge of the fender painted white, no doubt to make it more visible at night. (*Signal Corps*)

Right: France, 24 February 1945. The Dodge on the left bears a tonnage plate. A gas detection patch has also been painted on the hood. (*Signal Corps*)

Below: Italy, ambulances of the 316th Medical Battalion of the 91st Infantry Division. The ambulance in the background has the tonnage marking painted on the front right-hand bumper. The vehicle in the foreground has a makeshift roof rack. (*National Library of Medicine*)

French markings

France's armed forces were massively equipped with Dodge ambulances, especially the First French Army and the Second Armored Division. The crews consisted of mainly female personnel. Nurses and ambulance drivers, all had to know how their vehicle functioned and was serviced. These women had an essential part to play during World War II within the medical teams of the French units.

In order to identify vehicles of the French contingent, and wanting to announce their nationality to all who saw them, crews got rid of American identification and registration markings. These were replaced by the consular or French flag in such a way as to identify the vehicles according to French standards. Each crew identified its vehicle with their unit's markings.

The vehicle's registration number was on the front bumper and on one or both rear bumpers. It was often preceded by the French flag. The inscription was painted white on a black background. The registration number consisted of six figures and always began with a 4.

The radiator grilles were painted with the red cross on a white background. This practice was seen on both American and French vehicles.

1ère Armée Française (First French Army)

The First French Army applied the consular flag to the hood of its vehicles. The caducei medical markings had the U.S. references deleted from their design or were removed completely.

They were replaced by the French flag. Sometimes the flag was orientated in the direction of travel. The American registration disappeared in favor of the French one.

Below: The French flag of the First Army; an unidentified marking was been painted over it.

Above: An ambulance from the First French Army, 531st Medical Company. The radiator grille has been painted with the red cross, the front of the hood has been given the TQM code and the French registration number is on the bumper (*Author*)

Above right: Another ambulance from the First French Army, 531st Medical Company. A breakdown? The markings on the bumper have been partly rubbed off. (*Author*)

Right: France, 17 August 1944. French crews getting ready to bivouac between Sainte-Maxime and Toulon following the invasion of southern France two days earlier. (*ACME*)

Below: The insignia of the 531e Compagnie Sanitaire (531st Medical Company), 27th Train, has been painted on the door. (*Author*)

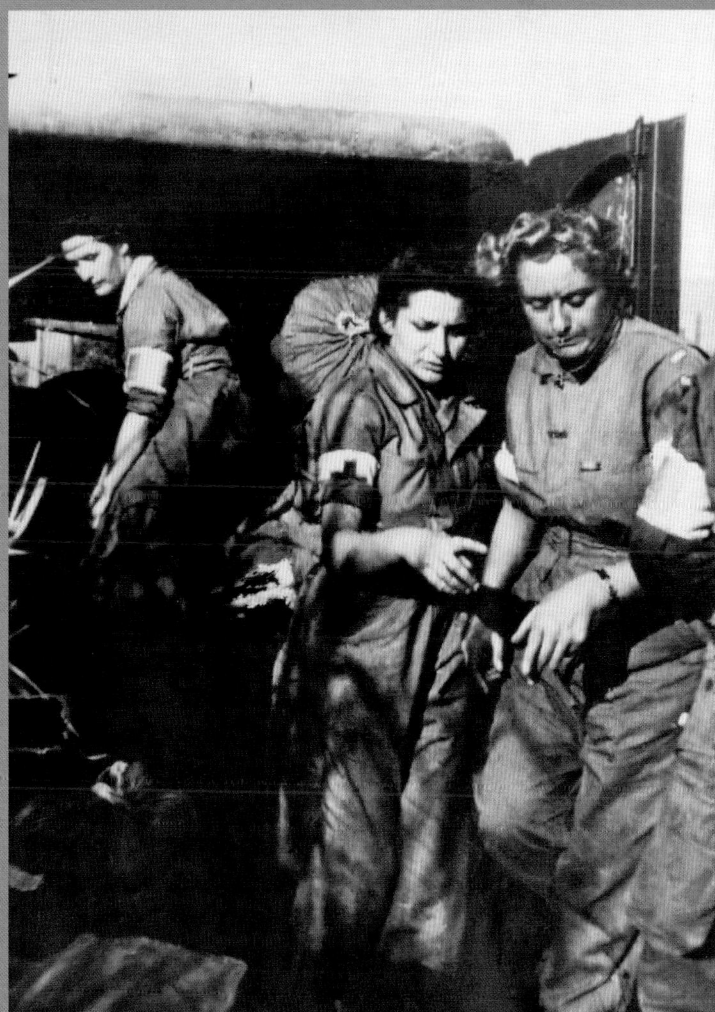

Deuxième Division Blindée (2nd French Armored Division)

The 2nd Armored Division (2e DB) also proceeded to get rid of the American inscriptions and apply the French flag and the unit's insignia. These markings were usually on the front doors. The caduceus was be replaced by the tactical insignia "S" specific to each company. Frequently, the ambulances of the "Rochambelles" had a name written on the front of the radiator grille.

This information concerning markings is given as a rough guide. Indeed, there were numerous variations for these markings because they were applied in the field in wartime. Anyone researching these vehicles and/or restoring one has to check for themselves in order to be able to deliver an accurate discourse or present a suitably restored vehicle.

Left: 531e Compagnie Sanitaire (531st Medical Company). The caduceus has simply been replaced by a French flag. (*Author*)

Below: Sainte-Maxime, France, 16 August 1944. Another field adaptation: note the stars. (*NARA*)

Above: Cerasuolo, Italy, 13 January 1944. An ambulance of the First French Army. On the rear door, the French registration is preceded by the French flag. The TQM code and the company prefix "F" can be seen in the top left corner of the door. (*Signal Corps*)

Right: France, 18 August 1944. 13th Medical Company of the 13th Battalion of the 2e DB. The American markings have been replaced by the French flag and the 2e DB insignia. The caduceus has been covered by an "S", designating a medical vehicle in the division. (*Signal Corps*)

Right: 531e Compagnie Sanitaire. Note the consular flag on the hood. The registration number is preceded by a French flag. (*Author*)

Below: Livorno, Italy, 9 January 1945. Peninsular Base Section markings on the rear bumpers. (*NARA*)

Above: An example of a nickname on an ambulance. (*NARA*)

Right: Italy, February 1944. "Caution Left Hand Drive" and "No Signal" markings.

Below: Scotland, 1944. The recognition markings have been painted over. The warning "Caution, No Signal, Left Hand Drive" has been recently applied to the rear door. (*NARA*)

Aerial shot of the 198th General Hospital in Paris; the vehicles have hood stars and small stars on the doors. (*National Library of Medicine*)

Southern France, August 1944. The vehicle has circled stars on the hood, roof and doors; this was a common practice in the field.

Above: In the Pacific. An ambulance in a very rare camouflage scheme. (*NARA*)

Above right: Italy, 262nd Station Hospital. The front doors of the ambulance have been painted with a red cross. This was an exceptional practice.

Right: An original marking on the front door. This could be a storage or de-storage marking.

Right below: Personalized marking, certainly a nickname: "OUTSIDE" or "OUTSIDER." It's a rather odd name for an ambulance. "Outsider" refers to anybody in a competition who has little chance of winning but who could nonetheless win.

Below: USA, 1944. The first ambulance is certainly a WC54. It's a vehicle of the Army Service Force, being used to transport wounded. The Army Service Force was one of the three autonomous components of the U.S. Army during World War II, the others being the Army Air Force and the Army Ground Force. They were created on 28 February 1942. (*National Library of Medicine*)

Above: England, April 1944. These ambulances are waiting for aircraft to return. The lead vehicle has received new markings which cover the word "Ambulance" on the front roof. Note the tip of the identification star on the roof of some of the ambulances. (*NARA*)

Above left: June 1944, England. The pane on the rear door has been partly covered by the red cross. (*NARA*)

Left: Negros, Philippines. This ambulance has been entirely repainted in order to remove all of its markings. (*NARA*)

Below: New Guinea. These ambulances have had their red crosses covered to make them less visible. (*NARA*)

Above: Luzon, Philippines. The markings have been completely painted over. Only a dark little red cross has been applied.

Right: England, summer 1944. This ambulance has a side cross overlapping onto the roof, most certainly to simplify positioning and to avoid going around the shape of the fender. (*NARA*)

Below: Angaur Islands, Palau. This red cross does not follow the instructions. The white background goes down to the rounded wheel arch and fender. (*NARA*)

Above: Germany, 27 April 1945. Freed American and British PoWs heading to a rear base to be evacuated. They are being transported by the 9th Troop Carrier. "Caution" and "Max speed" have been applied to the top of the ambulance. (*NARA*)

Left and opposite top: Sicily, 25 July 1943. The ambulances in the background have a simple star on each side. This is non-regulation, most certainly quickly done away with. (*NARA*)

Right: England. An uncommon combination of markings. The vehicle has retained the inscription "Ambulance" but has the two big red crosses of the final style of markings. (*NARA*)

67061A

UNITED STATES ARMY
BORBORY

Above: A convoy of American ambulances paused in Germany.

Right: Ambulance in Italy.

Above: Medical men of the 391st Bomb Group, in England.

Left: Medical Captain Graham, with cap, England.

AMBULANCE
AMBULANCE
AMBULANCE
AMBULANC

Guam, 1945. These ambulances are waiting for wounded personnel from the Battle of Okinawa. The vehicles have no white stars. The marking "U.S. ARMY" can be seen on the doors. One can also discern ambulances with light roofs. These are probably U.S. Navy vehicles. *(NARA)*

6 Postwar and Reconstruction

From 1943 onwards, the French materiel service adopted the American Ordnance Service model. The first contact between the authorities from the Matériel Department and American experts took place in Tunisia during February 1943. This allowed the way the Ordnance Service worked to be studied and how American materiel would be supported once delivered with the possible opening of a front in Italy.

With their superiority in all domains, despite their troops' flagrant lack of experience, the underlying American pressure at the Cherchell Conference (Algeria) in October 1942 emerged during the Anfa (Casablanca) Conference in January 1943 when the Americans confirmed they did not want to equip the Free French Forces. In reality, the two parties benefited from the plan since they merged on 1 August 1943 to give birth to the new French Army under General Giraud.

It was initially planned as 12 divisions split into two armies (one with three infantry divisions, one with four and three armored divisions) and an army corps with one infantry division and a detachment of one armored division (the future 2nd Armored Division, 2e DB). Under pressure from the Allies, these 12 divisions were reduced to 11 then eight, made up of five infantry and three armored divisions. French disappointment did not end there. At the beginning of 1944, when the first materiel was delivered, the Americans pressured French command for its larger units to adhere to American forces' standards. Indeed, deliveries of materiel were made by "lots," from the simple vehicle to supplying a large unit. The French command, however, disregarded American pressure.

Without notice, the Americans stopped supply. The French command submitted and had to disband divisions in the process of being formed, like the 3e DB or the 6e DIM (Division d'Infanterie Motorisée), so it could align itself to the American standards, and form backup units following the Ordnance Service standards, and get the necessary certifications that would make the larger units operational. Thus it was that the 1re DB was only homologated when its group of repair squadrons (11e GER) was joined by a third repair squadron (ER), which was taken from the 14e GER in the disbanded 3e DB (which only had one such unit anyway).

France, after the war, was poor. Once the joys of liberation were over, the harshness of life returned. The country was rebuilding and had to make an intense effort. The Marshall Plan helped this renaissance. For the Army, the situation was also difficult. The units suffered from dilapidated premises and disinterested personnel who, after winning the war, went back home.

In 1948, when the ERGM (Etablissements de Réserve Générale de Matériel) was created at Clermont-Ferrand, a production line for rebuilding the Dodges was set up. Its "automobile" calling was confirmed at the beginning of the 1950s when it became the "established brand" for small trucks in the tactical range and light four-wheel-drive vehicles.

The vehicles taken in by the ERGM were generally completely stripped down. Damaged items were replaced or repaired. Ambulance bodywork was often repaired by fitting sheet metal over damaged areas. The front doors were often replaced by doors with full-pane glass, easy to use and needing fewer parts. The leatherwork was replaced by new or partly renewed material. Mechanical components were serviced or replaced with parts from vehicles thought to be beyond repair. Once restored, the ambulances were assigned to the military or sold on the civilian market. The fire service thus obtained vehicles which were used as ambulances, emergency or fire vehicles.

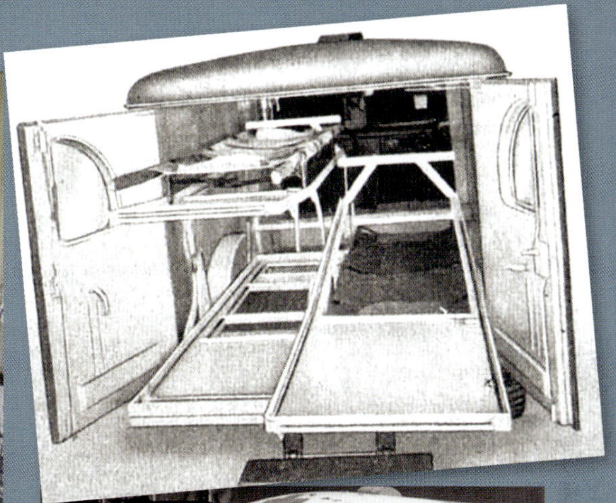

Above left: The inside of a WC54 which went through ERGM in 1966. The body is white; only the instrument panel has kept its olive drab paint. The stretcher mountings have been modified by the reconstruction workshops. The door windows have been replaced with the full-pane model.

Above right and top right: A Swiss Army ambulance in 1960. It has been considerably modified.

Left: Between 1946 and 1954, the registration numbers of military vehicles used in Indochina began with "IC" (*Infanterie Coloniale*).

Below: The plate applied by ERGM, giving the chassis number, the date it left ERGM, and the model. The instructions on the plate are a condensed version of the American ones.

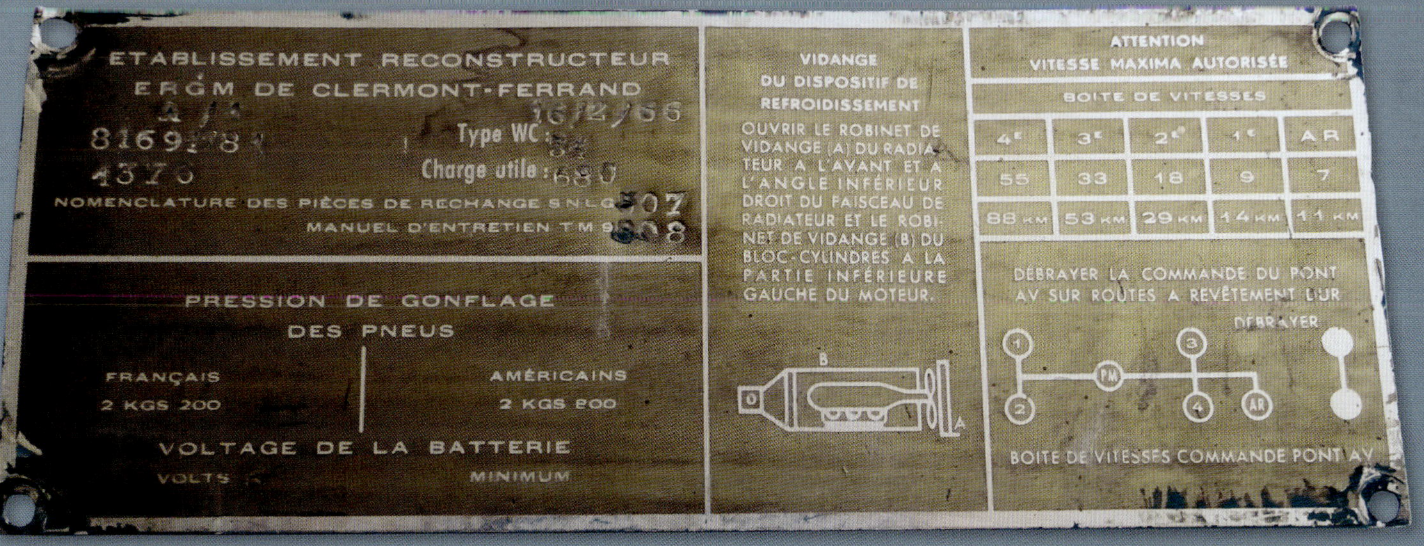

Above: Japan, 12 September 1945. Ambulances waiting on a Japanese airfield. (*Signal Corps*)

Above: Patients being transferred from aircraft to waiting ambulances. (*National Library of Medicine*)

Above: Luxembourg, 25 December 1944. A damaged ambulance from the 5th Medical Battalion of the 5th Infantry Division. It has an extra blackout light on the right fender. (*NARA*)

Left: 1945. A driver poses in front of his ambulance. (*National Library of Scotland—The Portal to Texas History*)

Opposite: Germany, 1945. (*National Library of Scotland—The Portal to Texas History*)

2004-103-157

Above: 10th Field Hospital, Orléans, France. Several tents have been pitched in the middle of a forest. A sign bearing the name of the hospital is near the row of parked ambulances. (*National Library of Medicine*)

Opposite: An ambulance from the First French Army, 531st Medical Company. The radiator grille has been painted with the red cross, the front of the hood has been given the TQM code and the French registration number is on the bumper. (*Author*)

Left: 531st Medical Company. The ambulance still bears American recognition markings. The crew has most certainly just received the vehicle as a replacement. (*Author*)

Opposite top: 1942. The view from a Dodge WC27 of the British Eighth Army as a column of German PoWs files past. (*American Field Service*)

Opposite below: Belgium, early January 1945. An ambulance destroyed near the edge of Bastogne. (*NARA-Medical Department*)

Above: Probably Pearl Harbor, Hawaii Territory. These WC54 ambulances, lined up on the quayside, are waiting for wounded from the aircraft carrier USS *Intrepid.* (*Signal Corps*)

Left: Seventh Army, Sainte-Maxime sector, France, 16 August 1944. This medical company is in a field where stakes have been placed to prevent glider landings. (*Signal Corps*)

Opposite: Normandy, France, 6 June 1944. LCT 535 transporting a field hospital unit to Omaha Beach.

Above: 50th Field Hospital, June 1944. (*National Library of Medicine*)

Opposite top: Ambulances of the 430th Medical Battalion being serviced by the 596th Ambulance Company motor pool, 24 March 1945. (*NARA*)

Opposite below: Roosevelt Field, Long Island, New York, 24 March 1945. A demonstration of how wounded are loaded onto a WACO glider. (USAAF)

DANGER
GASOLINE

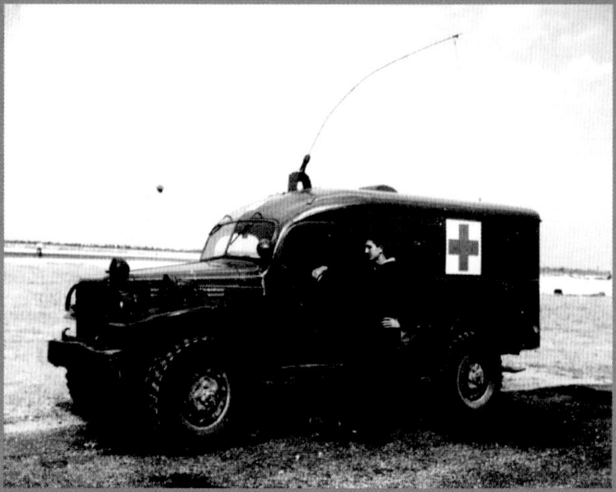

Above: Naval Air Station, Fort Lauderdale, Florida, August 1944. This ambulance has been given radio equipment for use as a radio relay on the air base. (*NARA*)

Left: England, 18 July 1944. This ambulance from the 303rd Bomb Group is equipped with a two-way radio for communication with the control tower. Even equipped this way, the vehicle retains its primary function as an ambulance. (*NARA*)

Above: Germany, 1945. An ambulance in front of a 19th-century building transformed into a hospital. Two soldiers are transporting a casualty on a stretcher to the building's entrance. (*National Library of Medicine*)

Right: New Georgia, 1943. (*NARA—USMC*)

Opposite below: Luxembourg, 1945. A view of the front of a country house serving as a medical center. Snow has covered the yard. The rear door of the ambulance nearest the house is open and personnel are moving between it and the building. Note the various items tied down on the second vehicle. (National Library of Medicine)

Left: England, 6 March 1944. An early model of ambulance with its tool rack on the left-hand side and a small filler cap. Its registration number has been painted on the rear doors as the visible "USA" suggests. (*NARA*)

Below: France, 18 April 1945. These ambulances of the 9th Troop Carrier are waiting on the le Bourget ramp to evacuate the wounded to hospitals. The shipping marking is not on all the vehicles. (*NARA*)

Above: Saipan, 1944. An example of a jerry can mounted on the fender. (*NARA*)

Right: Italy, October 1944. This later model of ambulance with the big filler cap retains the smaller identification markings. (*NARA*)

Left: Oahu, Hawaii. Dodge WC54s and a WC21 side by side on the tarmac of Hickam Field. They were assigned to Air Transport Command whose mission was to respond to emergency requests from American military bases throughout the world. (*NARA*)

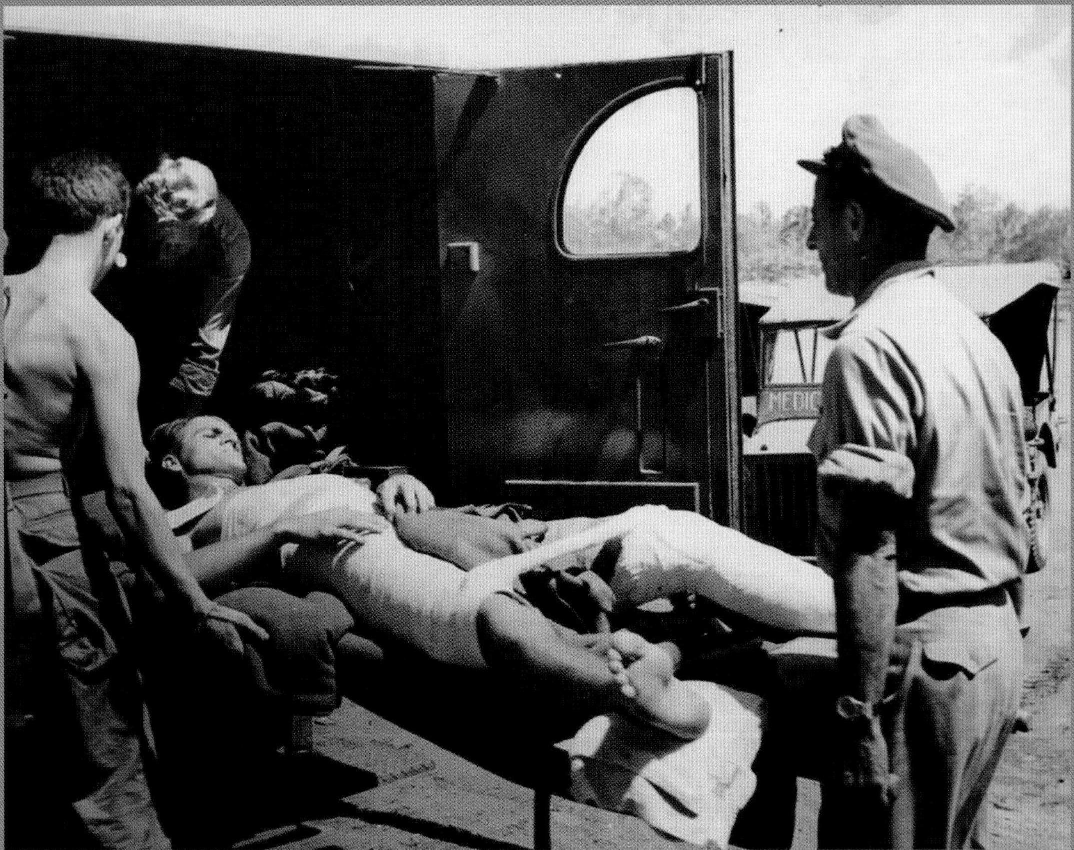

Right: New Guinea, July 1944. This photo shows clearly the rear door seals. On the top of the rear door is the triangular seal. The wooden stretcher stop can also be seen. (*NARA*)

Right: Poltava U.S. airfield, Russia, 12 January 1945. The wintry conditions in Russia obliged the crew to fit snow chains. These were part of the on-board equipment and were stored in the boxes in the body. (*NARA*)

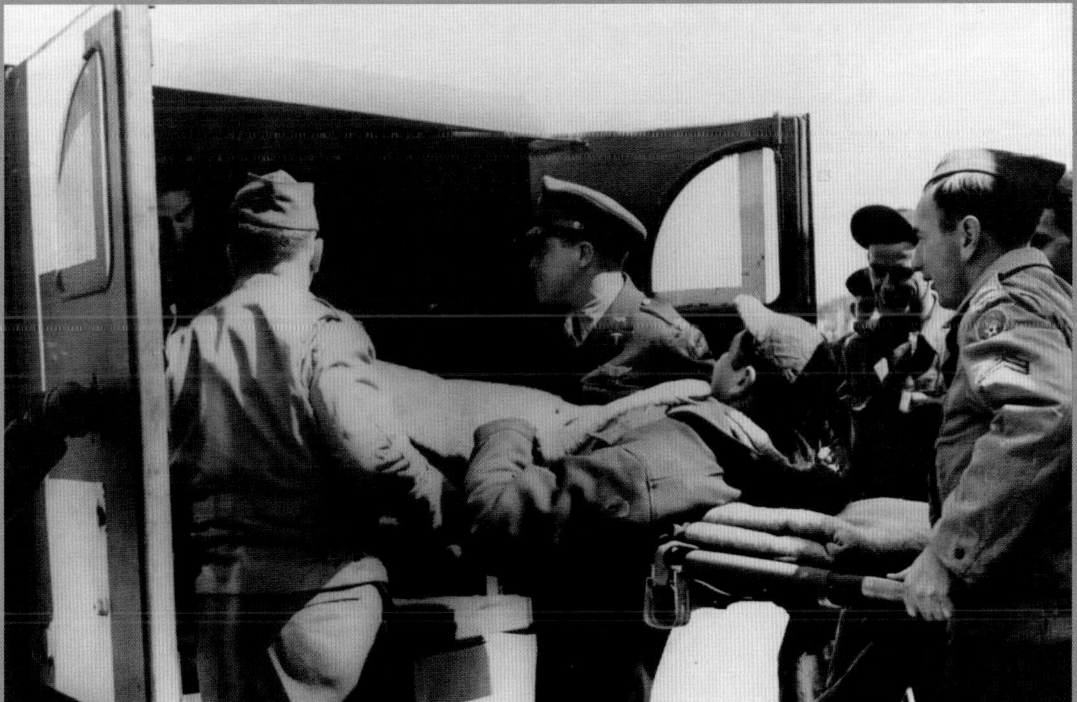

Left: The pane of the rear door is partly covered by the red cross. (*NARA*)

Above: Solomon Islands. An example of registration markings on the rear doors. (*NARA*)

Left: An example of the medical gear equipping the ambulances. This is a splint kit with accessories. (*NARA*)

Right: India/Burma, March 1944. The correct shape of caduceus in its regulation place. (*NARA*)

Below: England, June 1944. The wounded are evacuated on their return from a bombing raid over Germany. This rear view enables us to see the rear door seals. (*NARA*)

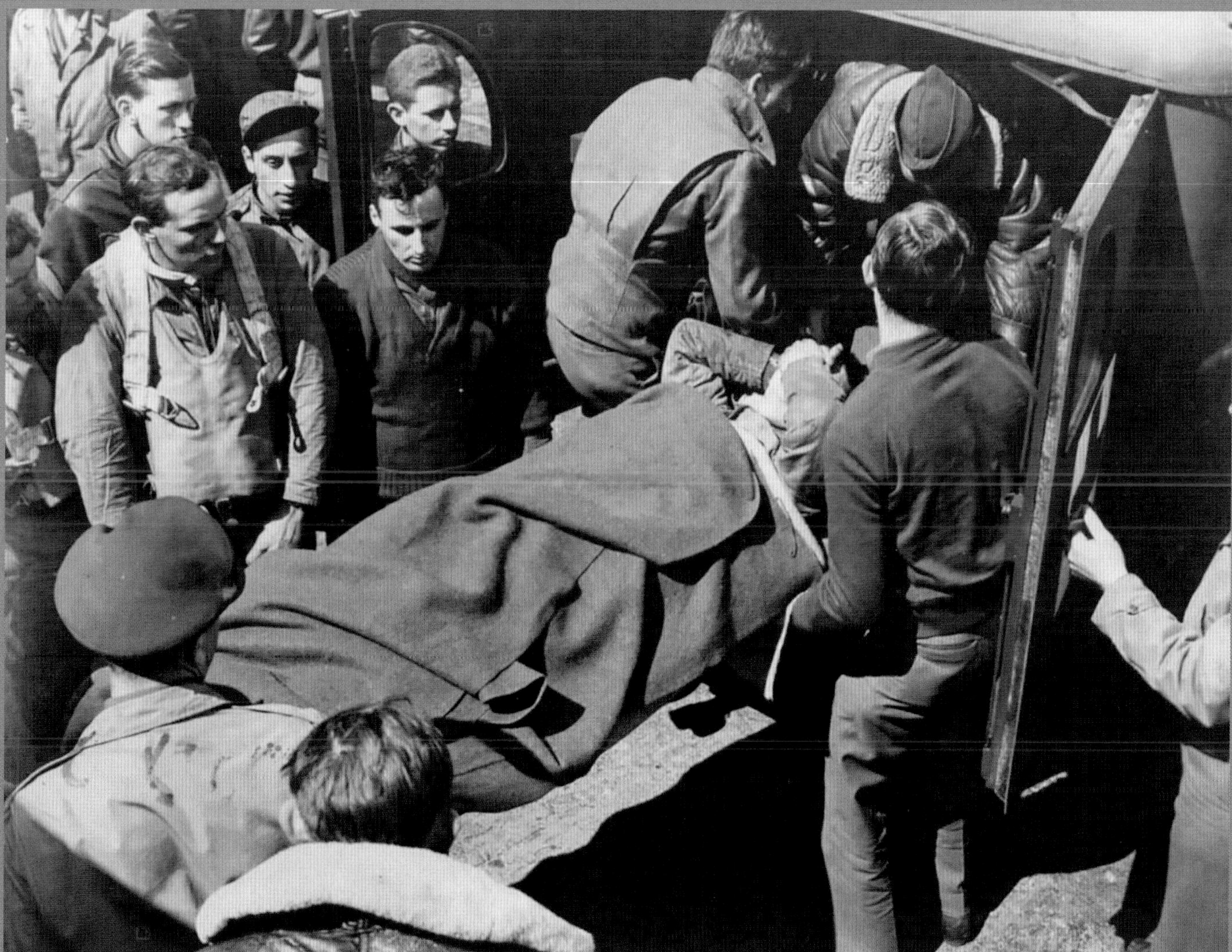

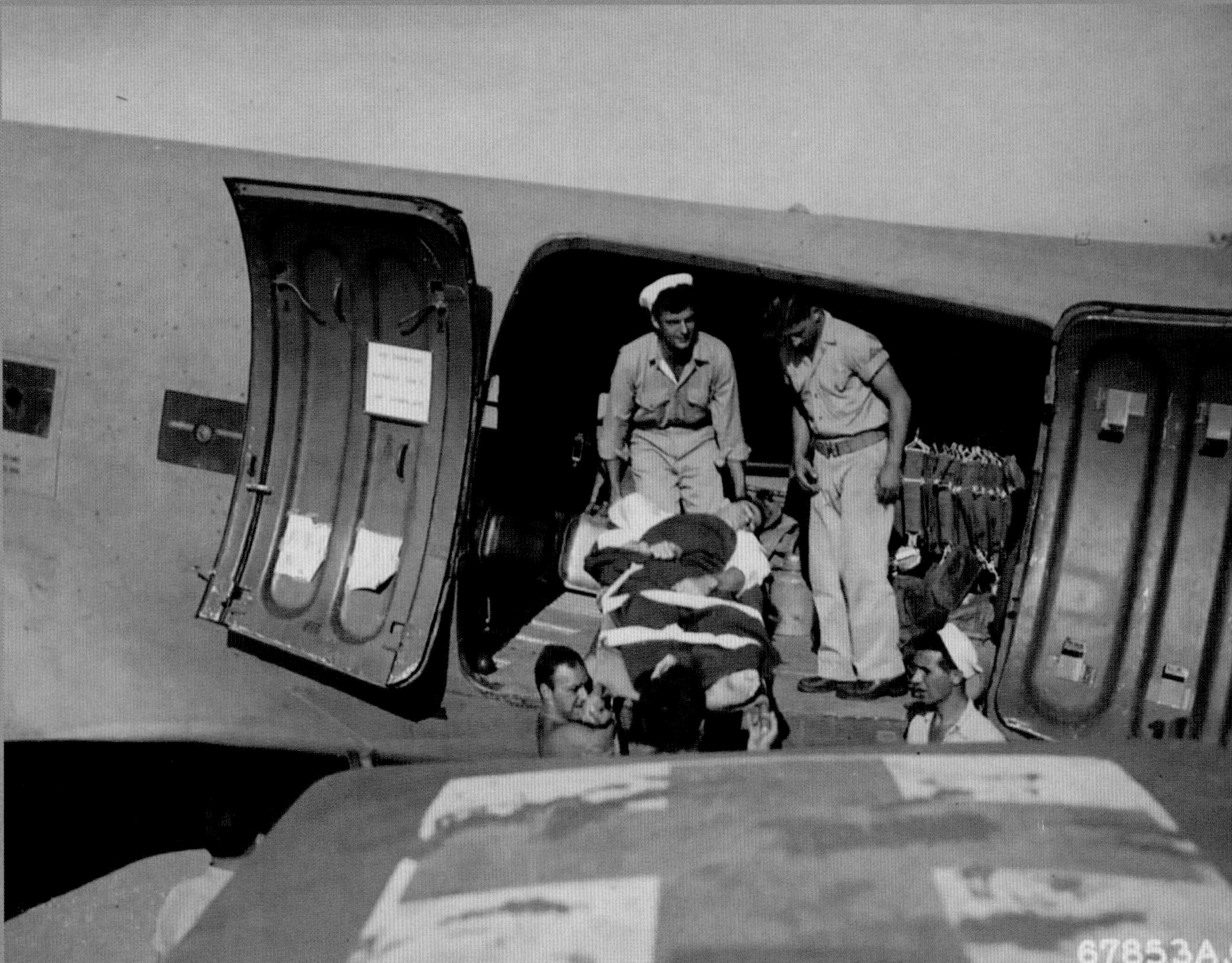

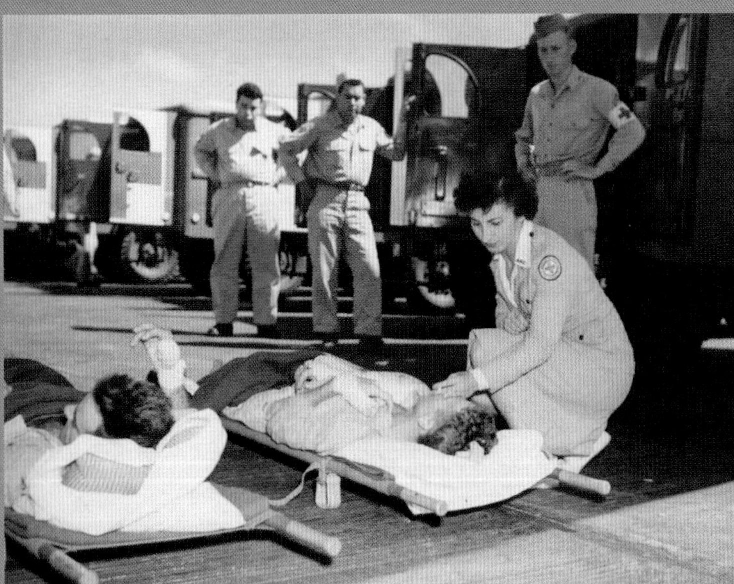

Above: Solomon Islands, March 1944. This shot of the roof shows the details of the first style of cross, worn and dirtied by the weather. (*NARA*)

Left: Oahu, Hawaii. This nurse from the American Red Cross tends to her patients waiting to be evacuated. (*NARA*)

Right: Philippines. The footstep was useful as a seat and, as such, often left in the down position, ending up mangled after the vehicle backed into something. (NARA)

Below: Guam, July 1945. Despite the approaching end of the conflict, the ambulances do not have uniform markings. (*NARA*)

Above: Aircraft "Marishka" coming to a stop beside an ambulance in Italy, 1944. (*USAF*)

Below: Ambulances and C-47s in Germany. (USAF)

Bibliography

Military Manuals

M9-808, 31 January 1944
TM9-808B, 17 November 1944
TM9-2853, 7 July 1945
SNL G502, 1 December 1942
SNL G502, 1 May 1944
SNL G657
AR850-5
The Technical Service: The Ordnance Department: Procurement and Supply

Specialized Books

Becker, Emile, U.S. Army (ETO 1944–45) *Marquages et organisation*. Luxembourg: Becker et Milmeister, 1988.

Becker, Emile and Dentzer, Guy, *Dodge VC1–WC-64KD (1940–1945)*. Emile Becker, 1992.

Bouchery, Jean and Charbonnier, Philippe, *U.S. Army: Les marquages des véhicules 1944*. Histoire & Collections, 2018.

Véhicules Militaires Magazine. No. 56, April/May 2014.

Doyle, David, *The Development and Deployment of Dodge Military Trucks: 1940–1975*. Ampersand Publishing, 2015.

Lorrain, Dominique (Lieutenant-colonel), *Recueil des Structures du Matériel de l'Armée de Terre—des origines à 2017*.

Right: Officers and men of the 303rd Bomb Group look out from the control tower at an airfield in the UK, with ambulances standing ready in the foreground.

Below: Evacuation of wounded into aircraft.

Acknowledgments

I would like to thank my family and friends who, for all these years while I was restoring my Dodge WC54, supported and helped me in every situation, no matter how difficult.

I would like to thank my partner, Vicky Guétat, who backed me during the writing of this book and while restoring my Dodge WC54.

Thank you to my photographer, Gérard Guétat, for his numerous images that illustrate this book.

I would like to thank Alexandre Delbes for his help with certain references from the technical manuals or SNLs, and also Yoann Borsato, who pointed me in the right direction and helped me solve certain mysteries.

Thank you to all the people who enabled me to access such a great number of photos, some of which were unpublished, and who gave me some of their time. I would also like to thank the Surplus Militaires et Industriels for access to its pool of ambulances so I could carry out comparisons and record various details.

Finally, I'd like to thank *Ordnance Militaria* for their stencils for the Dodge's markings. Their website is at www.ordmilitaria.com.

Other Titles in the Casemate Illustrated Special Series:

U.S. ARMY AMBULANCES AND MEDICAL VEHICLES IN WORLD WAR II

by Didier Andres

A fully illustrated book covering all types of ambulances and medical vehicles used by the U.S. Army during World War II.

JULY 2020 | 9781612008653

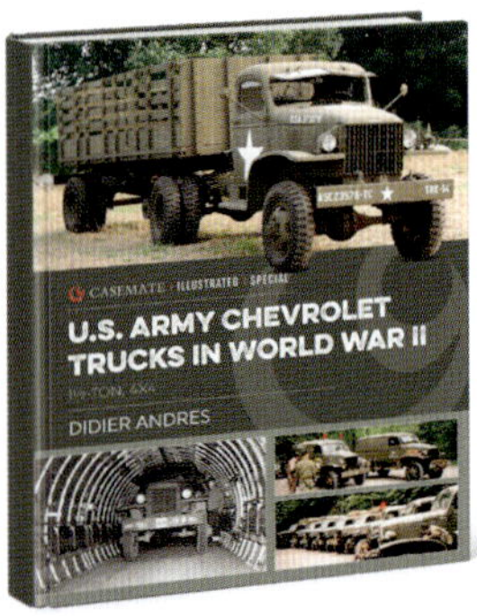

U.S. ARMY CHEVROLET TRUCKS IN WORLD WAR II

by Didier Andres

A fully illustrated and detailed account of the 1 ½-ton Chevy truck and its use by the U.S. Army during World War II.

MAY 2020 | 9781612008639

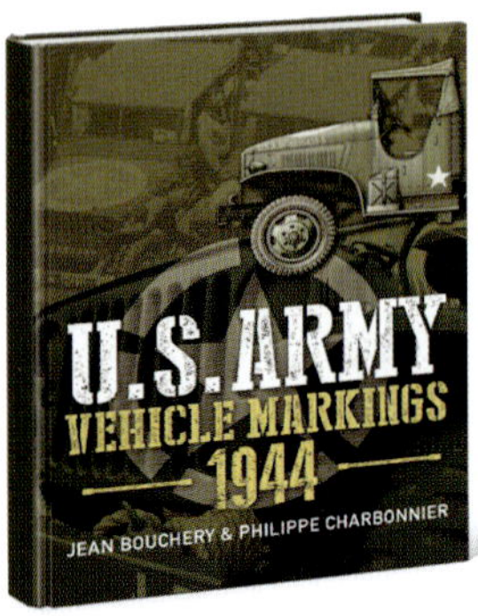

U.S. ARMY VEHICLE MARKINGS 1944

by Jean Bouchery and Philippe Charbonnier

The ultimate guide to the markings used on U.S. Army tanks, lorries and Jeeps in 1944, invaluable to historians, modelers and collectors.

JUNE 2019 | 9781612007373

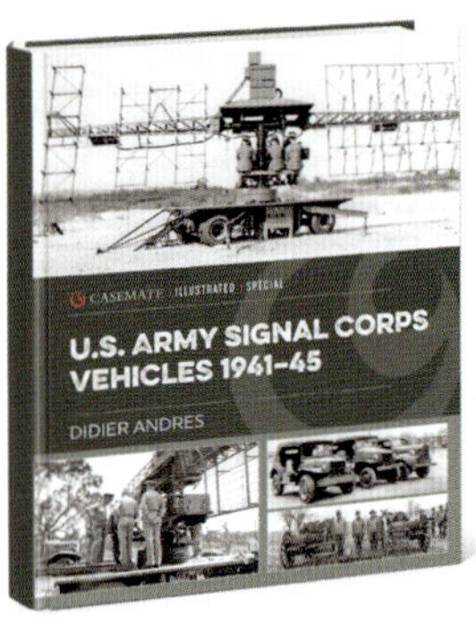

U.S. ARMY SIGNAL CORPS VEHICLES 1941–45

by Didier Andres

A comprehensive and fully illustrated account of all the vehicles needed to move, use, and maintain communications equipment vital to the success of the U.S. Army during World War II.

OCTOBER 2021 | 9781636240640